10 Terrific Parties

From Scuba Splash to Sixties Bash!

Naomi Black

PRICE STERN SLOAN
Los Angeles

A TERN ENTERPRISE BOOK

© 1990 by Tern Enterprise, Inc.

Published by Price Stern Sloan, Inc.
360 North La Cienega Boulevard, Los Angeles, California 90048

Printed in Singapore.

9 8 7 6 5 4 3 2 1

Library of Congress Cataloging-in-Publication Data

Black. Naomi. 1957–
    10 Terrific parties / by Naomi Black.
       p.   cm.
    ISBN 0-89586-782-6
    1. Entertaining. 2. Menus. 3. Cookery. I. Title
TX731.B57 1990   89-26935
642.4—dc20   CIP

Recognizing the importance of preserving that which has been written, Price Stern Sloan, Inc. has decided to print this book on acid-free paper, and will continue to print the majority of the books it publishes on acid-free paper.

10 Terrific Parties: From Scuba Splash to Sixties Bash
was prepared and produced by
Tern Enterprise, Inc.
15 West 26th Street
New York, New York 10010

Editor: Stephen Williams
Designer: Judy Morgan
Photography Editor: Ede Rothaus
Production: Karen L. Greenberg

Typeset by Mar+x Myles Typographic Services
Color separations by United South Sea Graphic Art Co., Inc.
Printed and bound in Singapore by Tien Wah Press (pte) Limited

ACKNOWLEDGMENTS

I'd like to thank all of the cooks who shared their recipes with me and allowed me to print them and, in some cases, adapt them. Some of them are professional cooks and caterers, others display their talents only to their fortunate friends, but each one is an impressive host in his or her own right:

Elizabeth Benvenutti, owner of Elizabeth Anne's catering in Pittsburgh, Pennsylvania

BB Bralower, wine consultant, of Roslyn, New York

Shamus Butler of Butler's Quarters Catering in Palenville, New York

Joanne Claus, owner of the Haydon House bed and breakfast in Healdsburg, California

Great Performances Catering of New York, New York

L'Habitation de Lonvilliers beach resort in St. Martin, French West Indies

Carrie Levin, co-owner of the Good Enough to Eat restaurants in New York, New York, and High Falls, New York

Roger Mufson, owner of Upstairs, Downstairs restaurant in Madison, Wisconsin

Miya Patrick, owner of The Charles Hinckley House bed and breakfast in Barnstable Village, Massachusetts

A tip of the hat, also, to Mary Forsell, Judy Habegger, Marian Rivman and John Bralower.

CONTENTS

CONTENTS

When reading accounts of parties in magazines and newspapers, I often come across the words drama and immortality, which suggests that the writers expect more than just good food and a comfortable environment when they go out. They want parties that will make history. Yes, a party should be recorded in one's personal annals of great events, but parties don't always have to be given on a grand scale. A small party fits where a larger gathering does not. A small party, depending on intimacy more than anything else, crystallizes a moment. Even without great drama, a small party can reach greatness through its sense of itself, by conveying a message of confidence, poise and contentment. Granted, a host may choose to set a dramatic scene, but the essence of the party will still be a small drama made complete by the people involved.

A host needn't invite guests who aren't well-liked to a small party. With a limited guest list, the host should invite only friends, or potential friends (because it's nice to occasionally invite a newcomer into the extended family).

How many people work best at a small party? It can depend on space, the occasion and the budget. Generally, however, six to eight guests is a prime number (no pun intended).

As for when to throw the party, I think parties are good 365 days a year. For this reason I've included a calendar that gives you a reason to have a party on every day of the year (see page 132). Use it to create your own party themes. You might have even more fun if you do a little digging to flush out the facts behind the date. A decent library will have plenty of resources to help you find out how a given holiday is celebrated in its country of origin, what kind of art or music a particular birthday boy or girl created or in what context an historical event occurred. In most cases, less than an hour's worth of research will provide you with plenty of ideas, background scenery, invitations and even food.

For example, you might want to serve hot dogs and soft pretzels on December 27, the day Radio City Music Hall opened in New York City; old movies recall that era and also give Christmas revelers a chance to sit down and relax. Invitations might be inspired by the Rockettes, an organ or the architecture of Radio City Music Hall itself.

Ink in dates that appeal to your sense of whimsy. The game plan is not to follow what's in this book exactly but to use the ideas as inspiration to create a personal, intimate party that suits you and your friends.

Finding a good recipe becomes one of the adventures of entertaining. All of us have cookbooks on which we rely, but the real fun of the recipe hunt lies in meeting other gourmands. This book reflects the wide variety of sources that are open to all cooks: friends and neighbors, restaurants and caterers and resorts and inns. Some of the recipes are from food professionals, some are from hosts who have a special touch. Other recipes were my own creation. Feel free to pick and choose among these sources, and be sure to follow your own instincts when hosting a small party.

With few exceptions, chefs are willing and usually delighted to share recipes with appreciative diners. You can expand your recipe collection and possibly your circle of friends by simply asking for the secret to a good dish at your favorite restaurant. I hope that you will see the recipes in this book as an extension of this philosophy. Bon appetit!

—Naomi Black

SHORT ONE EGG?

I admire cooks who scoff at planning ahead. They must never find themselves short one egg in the middle of a recipe or still chopping crudités when the guests arrive. For we imperfect humans, advance planning is a necessary evil, a bow to the hobgoblins of routine. One scatterbrained moment shouldn't tip the balance between success and disaster; but two or three can easily turn entertaining into a nightmare. By plotting shopping and cooking strategies beforehand, you *can* limit the possibilities of mishap.

Think of preparing a meal as a game, complete with tactics, forward and backward movement and chance. Tactics help you move in the desired direction and give you the confidence necessary to deal with the unpredictable.

Once you've settled on a game plan and have reassured yourself it's workable in terms of time and the pocketbook, you'll need to make master lists for shopping and chores, from polishing silver to hiring a babysitter.

THE PERFECT NUMBER

The respected food writer M.F.K. Fisher in her book *An Alphabet for Gourmets* recalls a walk during which she and her companion discussed The Perfect Meal: "We decided, after some fumbling and confusion, that time, place, weather and, above all, people were as important to the gastronomical consummation as the food itself. We settled on six as the perfect number of guests, including our two selves of course."

Another woman of great drama, Lillian Hellman, agreed in part: "Sit-down dinners are often only good for six to eight people," she wrote in *Eating Together: Recollections and Recipes*. Scaled down, a dancing party or cocktail party brings out a jolliness missing at many larger fetes.

Initial Planning

Checklists won't help if you don't have an overall picture of what needs to be done. In short, you must plan the type of party you want, decide on a menu, shop (sometimes more than once), cook, clean house and have it all done at least half an hour before guests knock at the front door. The lists provided in this chapter are by no means exhaustive, yet they include a longer roster than you'll probably need. Pick and choose from among them to come up with your own master list, which will inevitably change with each type of party you give.

By choosing to give a small party, you've already passed "Go." The next few items to tackle focus on what *kind* of small party you want.

Formal vs. Informal

The consensus among most modern etiquette experts is that formal dinner parties should be served by someone other than the hosts. In terms of the average American, however, who works by day and entertains by night, *formal* has also come to include an elegant party that calls for the use of good silver and china, no matter who serves or what the guests are wearing. In fact, you can use contrasts to your advantage to make a party unusual. For example, for a different approach to a picnic, set your best china outside on a freshly washed area rug topped by a lacy tablecloth, or plan a sumptuous midnight buffet for overnight guests and ask everyone to dress in their best pajamas (it helps to have a fireplace).

Invitations

One of the major differences between a small party and a larger gathering has to do with the invitations. At affairs with more than a dozen people, it's likely that some potential guests will decline the invitation or be waylaid at the last minute, so you should invite more people than you actually want at the party. For sit-down dinners and smaller celebrations, extend your invitation only to as many people as you can truly handle and ask that your invitees respond with their confirmation. (Make it clear whether your guests may bring a friend or spouse along.)

Have fun with your invitations. Small parties lend themselves to special touches, either handmade invitations or, if you want to go all out, special delivery, which does not necessarily mean through the mail. An account manager for a prestigious hotel group in Manhattan knew she had to catch the attention of the press for a special occasion, so she sent a startling invitation. A messenger hand-delivered a live goldfish to each hoped-for guest, emptying the fish into a small glass bowl before he rang each doorbell. The response was incredible.

You needn't go to such extremes, but with a little thought and ingenuity you can certainly come up with something remarkable. Try making personalized jack-in-the-boxes; set a wrapped "present"—with an invitation inside a box that is inside a box—outside people's doors; or with the help of spouses or a little sneakiness on your part, leave invitations in friends' refrigerators for them to find once you're gone.

Although the tradition of inviting equal numbers of men and women to a sit-down dinner has become more relaxed in some parts of the country, the "rule" is based on some common sense that should influence all of your fetes: Aim for an interesting blend of friends of both sexes and various professions, political bents and ages. The designer and socialite Carolina Herrera was quoted in *Vogue* magazine as saying, "At the small dinners, one must take care with the guest list, because this house is too small to have more than one bore."

INITIAL PARTY PLANNING LIST

On what date will you give the party?

Does it conflict with other celebrations?

What theme or occasion will you celebrate, if any?

Will it be formal or informal?

How many guests do you want to invite?

What is your budget for the party?

How much time do you have to prepare, cook, serve and clean?

Will you use mail-order or take-out foods?

Do you want to hire a caterer or ask a friend to help?

Do you have all the equipment you'll need?

Do you have the space for the party you envision?

Be Realistic

Whether you plan a formal dinner or a casual brunch, remember your game plan. Keep to your budgets for time and money. If you find yourself wanting to stretch the limits, don't. Instead, stretch your imagination. (Try a less precious fish as a substitute for salmon or swordfish; use fresh herbs to liven up chicken; or plan a potluck party.) It's better to have ample amounts of inexpensive food than to serve a rare item that leaves tummies growling. An easy compromise is to garnish simple dishes with a treat—baked fish with a shrimp on top or salad with asparagus.

When estimating your time, be sure to include pre-party preparations: house cleanup, finding and testing infrequently used appliances, polishing silver or washing serving dishes, ironing tablecloths and the like. These small details often delay the larger chores, which can delay the shopping and cooking. The domino effect has its place in entertaining as well as in world politics.

The Master Schedule

After the initial planning, you're ready to play the game. Choose a sufficiently varied menu—combine light dishes with heavy ones, spicy with mild, simple with extravagant. One rule, however, deserves never to be broken: Do all your experimenting on a quiet evening alone or with a pal who won't mind pizza if the new dish doesn't work. Don't test kitchen experiments on treasured guests.

One handy hint can save some embarrassment: Jot down friends' allergies or dietary restrictions on a sheet in your basic cookbook. Even if you know the people well, you may easily forget their special needs, and a quick peek at your list before planning the menu will put it all in perspective.

Once the menu is set, read through the recipes and make up a full-menu list of ingredients side by side with a list of possible serving dishes and any unusual kitchen equipment you'll need to find. When devising the ingredients list, don't leave out items you *know* you have. (These inevitably disappear the day before the party.) Include everything, combining where necessary (for instance, 6 tablespoons of butter for the fish, 3 tablespoons for the bread, ¼ cup for the dessert, plus some to have on hand for bread and butter).

Compare the list to what is in the cupboard and refrigerator, being certain to check the amounts in the containers. Some items, of course, will be long gone by the day of the party, so you must account for your family's tastes and habits. Set aside the ingredients you'll need so they don't get gobbled up before the party (and do a quick double check before you start cooking). Don't forget to include on the shopping list snacks, alcoholic and nonalcoholic beverages and mixers and any other items you don't have an official

© Burke/Triolo

recipe for (like olives or ice cream), but plan to serve.

The next step is to draw up a master plan—in this case, a cooking, shopping and chores schedule. The recipes in this book give you a good idea of what can be prepared ahead of time and what has to be done at the last minute. You may feel a bit like a kindergartner following my tips for success, which require a magic marker and colored pens. But you can adapt the style of the schedule to whatever suits you, just as long as it is efficient and useful.

First, on a large sheet of paper (an inexpensive sketch pad

does the trick), write in the categories horizontally across the top of the page: *In advance; 5 to 7 days ahead; 3 to 4 days ahead; 2 days ahead; The day before; The day of the party; A few hours before; Right before the party.* If it's easier, use the actual dates that correspond to the categories.

Now comes the fun. Fill in each category with everything that you must do beforehand, from issuing invitations to opening red wine in advance to let it breathe. Use a different color pen for each type of task; everyone organizes their world in a slightly different manner, but the following gives you a general idea: green for shopping trips, black for recipe preparation, red for telephone calls, and purple or light blue for cleaning house, washing dishes and other general chores.

As time passes and you complete each job, draw a single line through the notation with a black magic marker or check it off on the lefthand side of the column. If all this seems silly for a small party, remember that a party of any size requires organization and sometimes the preparatory work that goes into a small party equals that of a larger one.

This sample master schedule resembles a list of impossible tasks given the hero in a fairy tale; many of the chores apply only to formal parties. Use the master list as a memory jog. Be more specific where you need to be. For instance, I note when I'm going to cook each recipe (or each stage of the recipe if they're at different times) and I fill in the details for exactly what I need to buy for the decor.

As a casual alternative to long, drawn-out preparation, invite your friends and plan the menu in advance, then do all the shopping and cooking in one or two days. Organization still functions as a basic building block; in fact, it may be the keystone that keeps you from falling apart.

The Unexpected

If you shrink back in horror when the dreaded Unexpected Guests come to the door, you must gather your strength and do what seems contrary to every bone in your body: Invite them in, even if you have bare pantries, nothing to drink or, even worse, a messy house.

One of the greatest advantages of becoming adept at giving small parties is that you learn that you can entertain in spite of disaster or a shortage of party food in your home.

Welcome your guests, first and foremost; they are, presumably, your friends. (I'm assuming, of course, that if you absolutely can't entertain, you will tactfully explain so.)

Fall back on any number of solutions. If you really must finish a chore, clean up or make a phone call just as your guests arrive, tactfully send them out to get ice, take-out food or some small item that will get them out of the house, not burden them too much and make them feel useful and welcome. If lack of food is a problem, call a reliable take-out place (a good host knows at least one and has its phone number at hand) or propose a healthy walk, stopping, of course, at a supermarket, delicatessen or gourmet shop.

Many kitchens lend themselves to conversation. If you have only two or three guests, you might even invite them into the kitchen and set them to work chopping, peeling or stirring. More company requires *you* to make the move in most cases. Invest in a simple tray with low sides, large enough to fit a cutting board, a few vegetables and a knife. Even better, look for a lap table that has three sides; this allows you more space to cut without banging your wrist. Bring the tray into the area where you'd like your guests to gather and chop away while you talk.

THE MASTER SCHEDULE

IN ADVANCE

Call calligrapher, typesetter or engraver for invitations and other party necessities, or buy them.

Send out invitations or telephone guests.

Make shopping list.

Place food orders with mail-order, caterer or take-out businesses.

Test any electrical equipment you will need.

Make a list of all equipment you may need to buy, borrow or rent.

Reserve rental equipment, plan shopping trips or confirm availability of items to borrow.

Plan centerpiece and other decor and furniture arrangement. Plan entertainment.

5 TO 7 DAYS AHEAD

Shop for pantry items, frozen foods, canned goods and ingredients to make dishes in advance.

Prepare whatever dishes possible this far in advance.

Check liquor supply and frequently used items, and add whatever is necessary to shopping list.

Order flowers.

Buy candles or other decor items.

Make sure table linens are clean.

Select your party clothes and launder or dry-clean them, if necessary.

Have menu and place cards delivered or written.

3 TO 4 DAYS AHEAD

Polish silver; clean seldom-used dishes.

Make sure glassware is not dusty or streaked.

Do major house-cleaning tasks.

Confirm all hired help.

Confirm all equipment to be brought in.

Make any food that can be frozen or will keep until the day of the party.

2 DAYS AHEAD

Clean house.

Make the seating plan.

Confirm flower delivery.

Prepare whatever dishes you can at this stage.

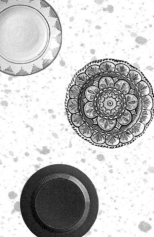

Buy ice.

Make sure you have all the ingredients you need except those that should be purchased at the last minute.

THE DAY BEFORE	THE DAY OF THE PARTY	2 HOURS BEFORE THE PARTY	JUST BEFORE THE PARTY
Finish as much of the cooking as possible.	Recheck supplies of anything that may have been consumed.	Arrange the flowers and final decor.	
Rearrange furniture where necessary.	Refrigerate white wine and other things to be chilled.		
Prepare room for guests' coats.	Place ashtrays and candles around the house.		
Set out umbrella stand.			
Set out fresh towels and soap.			Set out cheeses or non-perishable snacks.
Neatly write out or type instructions for caterers and serving help.			Open red wine and mix first batch of cocktails or juices.
Prepare sound system and select music.		Do last-minute cleanup.	Relax and get ready for a good time!
Set up bar.		Make room for dirty dishes.	
Iron linen.		Empty garbage.	
Set table.		Get dressed.	
Arrange all other dishes and flatware in order of use.			
Have coffee and tea service ready.			

THE LOOK OF THE MEAL

Cooks all over have recently begun to pay serious attention to color and presentation of food. Some gourmands think the trend to display food artfully has in some cases gone too far. But the extremes are settling into what appears to be a sensuous return to beautifully executed, delicious meals.

When putting your food together in the kitchen, take a minute to examine your elements. Do you have the makings for a colorful plate? Can you arrange the food so it pleases the eye? Think about presentation from the initial planning stage on. You've decided to serve carrots. Do you want them pureed, julienned, turned, in chunks, in coins? One handy reference, *Foodstyle* suggests making carrot flowers, ribbons and roses as well as using aspic cutters on parboiled carrots to make stars or other cutout shapes.

Draw ideas from advertisements in magazines, restaurants and the world around you. Your child bringing in a bird's nest the day before a few friends come to dinner might inspire you to make edible nests by frying thin strips of potatoes in a small strainer. One popular cooking magazine asked chefs to prepare a dish based on a work of art. Whether you like Mondrian, Monet or Pollock, don't be shy with your imagination. Forget the old rule that you shouldn't play with your food. Make a party of it. Invite a couple of friends over and, using the same ingredients, have everyone put together a plate of food without looking to see what the others are doing. Interpretation in cooking is as important to the final product as interpretation in music. And like music, food preparation and presentation demand practice and dedication for best results.

The designer of this table took great care to ensure that her guests would be pleased by the look as well as the taste of the meal. Arranging the food to please the eye is an important part of hosting a great party.

© Burke/Triolo

Table Art

Because you're interested in giving *small* parties, invest in a few plate patterns. Without spending too much money, you can browse through rummage sales and antique shops, picking up odd pieces, forsaken yet beautiful. Who says every plate has to match? Put your own sets together from mismatched, one-of-a-kind plates, such as petite florals, textured fruit patterns, plates with gold accents or varying colors of Depression glass or Fiestaware.

The same goes for glassware. Select an intriguing mix of etched glasses or goblets with cut-glass stems or, if you have plain dishes, colored glasses. One friend, with lots of energy and a low entertaining budget, uses Mason jars as glasses and invites guests for sumptuous breakfasts or classic desserts. She makes delightful French toast topped with vanilla ice cream and the best Indian pudding I've ever tasted. Balancing budget and expertise, she's become a perfect hostess even without all the trappings of a dining room—fine glassware, pressed linens and the like.

At many parties centerpieces have gone by the wayside. But centerpieces can enhance a setting, playing off of the food or the party theme. Found objects, from advertising display items to wave-washed bottles make for interesting conversation and can fill in when cut-glass vases or fine porcelain aren't available. Try geodes or other minerals, driftwood, baskets, trays, figurines and food. Just keep in mind that at a small party, the centerpiece should be low, unobtrusive and unscented. Buffet tables, on the other hand, invite more drama. Tall flowers; whole branches of flowering apple, dogwood or forsythia; and multitiered epergnes look more at home in the rear of a table covered with food. The only caveat: Keep candles from hair and clothes.

Making Party Tapes

Because you've chosen to throw a small party, you won't have to worry much about setting up a dance floor. Just roll up the rugs and make sure that the music equipment is protected and far enough away from flailing arms and legs to survive any mishap. Records are prone to skip at the slightest vibration so switch to tapes and compact discs even if you have to borrow or rent a machine.

The idea of making a dance tape can be as fun or as frightening as the idea of going to a party. On the one hand, sitting down to tape a pile of records will have you looking forward to an evening of good music. On the other hand, you might get pretty nervous thinking about how one dud song on the top might stop people on the dance floor in their tracks. But try not to worry too much. You can't please everyone with every song.

You can take two approaches to putting together your dance tape. One is to try to fit like-minded songs together: all the early rock and roll on one tape; all the Afro-Caribbean on another; and all the slow-dance tunes on another for the end of the night. The other approach might be more interesting for you and your guests, but it requires much more thought: Create a tape that mixes styles and moods. You'll want to start out with music that brings people to their feet, that nudges them onto the dance floor without it being so noisy that it irritates the guests who want to stand around and talk.

Outdoor Lighting

Lighting becomes a special challenge outside. Light your party for effect *and* safety. Make sure all steps and areas of uncertain footing are lit before adjusting any mood lighting. If you plan to entertain often, permanent step lights or an electric outlet accessible for outdoor lighting make sense. The alternative, which is also less expensive, requires a little more care and creativity but not much else.

Many hosts float votive candles in pools or bowls of water to capture a romantic atmosphere. Use a thin plastic dish as the boat. Or you can devise a light pattern by setting out paper bag luminaria. With just a dozen brown-paper grocery bags, some wet sand, and a dozen votive candles, you can create a magical effect. Fill the bags one-fourth full with moist sand (wet enough to extinguish the candle flame if it burns down, but not so wet as to destroy the paper bag). Line your walkway with the bags, or set them out in a pattern, and then put a candle in the center of each—far enough from the edges of the bag so there won't be any fires.

There are alternatives to candles. You can buy outdoor torches from Smith and Hawken, Clapper's or Lost City Arts (see Sources, pages 138 to 139). Or, if you have outdoor electric outlets, hang white Christmas lights from interestingly shaped bushes or low trees. In general, light from the ground up; the effect is softer and more pleasing than light from a makeshift spotlight.

THE PLEASURES OF THE TABLE

Jean-Anthelme Brillat-Savarin remains one of the more amusing characters in the world of gastronomy, though he lived in the nineteenth century. His anecdotes and scientific analyses on everything from appetite to thinness to sleep now seem both wonderfully dated and thought-provoking. Turning to what makes a good meal, the famed kitchen philosopher listed the following precepts:

Let the number of guests be not more than twelve, so that the talk may be constantly general;

Let them be chosen with different occupations but similar tastes, and with such points of contact that the odious formalities of introduction can be dispensed with;

Let the dining room be well lighted, the cloth impeccably white, and the atmosphere maintained at a temperature from sixty to seventy degrees;

Let the men be witty without being too pretentious, and the women charming without being too coquettish;

Let the dishes be few in number, but exquisitely choice, and the wines of the first quality, each in its class;

Let the service of the former proceed from the most substantial to the lightest, and of the latter, from the mildest to the most perfumed;

Let the progress of the meal be slow, for dinner is the last business of the day; and let the guests conduct themselves like travellers due to reach their destination together;

Let the coffee be piping hot, and the liqueurs chosen by a connoisseur;

Let the drawing-room be large enough to allow a game at cards to be arranged for those who cannot do without, yet still leave space for postprandial conversations;

Let the guests be detained by the charms of the company and sustained by the hope that the evening will not pass without some further pleasure;

Let the tea be not too strong, the toast artistically buttered, and the punch mixed with the proper care;

Let retirement begin not earlier than eleven o'clock, but by midnight let everyone be in bed...

In some ways very little has changed since Brillat-Savarin published these thoughts in *The Philosopher in the Kitchen* in 1825: We still look forward to a small party with good conversationalists in a comfortable room with good food and drink. We may not play cards after dinner, but we do still want—for lack of a better expression—to butter our toast artistically.

THE INGREDIENTS

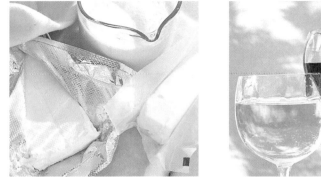 

Good planning should keep you from being short one egg in the middle of a recipe. Keeping a well-stocked pantry allows for impromptu get togethers without worry. Few of us can run out back and gather comestibles: wild asparagus, fresh berries and bark for black birch tea, not to mention tomatoes, cabbage and corn from the garden. Instead we must be content to stock the not-so-wild asparagus, and rely on interesting recipes and pretty presentations to dress up an unplanned party.

Small parties lend themselves to spontaneity. The spark that starts a last minute fête often ignites into an evening of successful fireworks. There is something special, a certain joyous combustibility, about a spontaneous gathering, but only if the host's enthusiasm is not dampened by mundane worries such as whether there's enough left in the kitchen to feed a small horde.

Many people say that you set yourself up for good luck; you build a foundation that lets you take advantage of a good situation when it passes by. In the same way, you set yourself up for an impromptu party by knowing that you have the makings for a few festive dishes tucked away in the pantry, refrigerator and freezer.

Pantry Staples

Although some of the pantry items listed below may be as familiar to you as turkey at Thanksgiving, a few made my list quite by accident. One sleety evening after I had been away from home for a few weeks, a friend popped in, eager to say hello and retreat from the nasty weather. After surveying my depleted stocks, I managed to assemble some chicken bouillon, cornmeal, dried sausage, onion and herbs into a reasonable one-pot meal.

Basic Staples

The cornmeal, which I hadn't used in ages, earned a respected place in my emergency pantry; it provides a ready ingredient for pancakes or muffins for breakfast, polenta or johnnycake for lunch or dinner and Indian pudding (with molasses) for dessert.

Another often-overlooked pantry staple is dried fruit, which makes an interesting addition to oatmeal. It works as an easy snack, and stewed it becomes a delicious accompaniment to meat or fowl. Horseradish, too, complements some fish and meat and can double as a sauce when you have no time or ingredients to prepare something more appropriate.

Use jams and jellies as dessert toppings; thin with juice, liqueur or both and heat on the stove to vary the consistency. If you've stashed some sweet dough in the freezer but have no fruit to fill a tart, turn to the tastiest jam you have, spread it on the dough, and make a criss-cross pattern of crust on top; the result is elegant yet simple.

Dried mushrooms help pasta sauces when fresh vegetables are a shopping trip away; or throw together a variation on the classic puttanesca sauce with anchovies, olives, capers and canned, peeled tomatoes. Sauté a red onion with some fresh basil and parsley from the garden, then add a dash of white wine and equal amounts of chopped olives and capers for quick crostini hors d'oeuvres as an alternative to canned pâté when you're in a pinch.

I admit to keeping on hand at least one can of whole asparagus spears at all times to share with my close friends (who admit to other close-to-the-heart favorites such as egg noodles and cottage cheese or peanut butter and banana sandwiches). Suffice to say, I bring out my mushy asparagus for tight deadlines and tight friends and eat it cold from the can. For real company, however, can the canned asparagus.

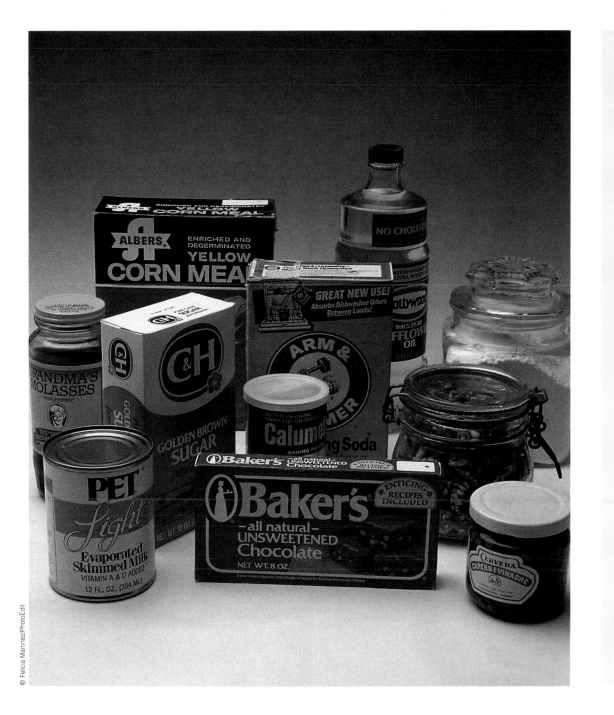

© Felicia Martinez/PhotoEdit

BASIC STAPLES

Continued

JAM, JELLY OR MARMALADE

LEMON JUICE

MAYONNAISE

MOLASSES

MUSTARD

NUTMEATS

OLIVES

PASTA

RICE

SOY SAUCE

TOMATO PASTE

VANILLA

WHOLE TOMATOES

WORCESTERSHIRE

YEAST

FRESH HERBS

BASIL

CHIVES

CORIANDER

DILL

GARLIC

MARJORAM

MINT

OREGANO

PARSLEY

ROSEMARY

SAGE

TARRAGON

THYME

Garden Herbs

If the idea of garden herbs raises a skeptical eyebrow or two, suspend your judgment. Starter kits (see Sources, pages 138 to 139) require about five minutes of initial work and produce fine plants even on New York City windowsills. The difference between having fresh herbs at your disposal and using dried herbs is like the difference between institutional food and a gourmet meal; although ostensibly the same, the end results are worlds apart.

Fresh Herbs

Start with basil and when in full leaf, this sweet herb will yield the gold that transmutes pine nuts to pesto, a sauce that itself can turn impromptu visits into entertaining successes. Pesto complements vegetables, pasta, chicken, poached fish, even scrambled eggs; the sauce freezes well, too, so it should be one of the first items on your list of freezer staples.

Thyme and parsley and rosemary, tarragon or marjoram usually fill out starter kits. All can be clipped and used simply with fish or chicken *en papillote*; and since you plan to dine with fewer than a dozen guests, windowsill cuttings tend to suffice. Small parties make it easier to garnish with garden-grown herbs, although sometimes you might rely on the supermarket if you're preparing a dish with large amounts of basil, dill or parsley.

Round out your herb garden with whatever strikes your fancy. A trip to a local herb farm or seed store tickles the imagination with rarer varieties such as opal and licorice basil, Mallorca rosemary, Greek oregano and lemon thyme.

Although not herbs technically, many people think of garlic and ginger in the same category. It's easier to buy garlic bulbs and fresh ginger at the supermarket; both should always be on hand.

© Walter Chandoha

The rosemary, sage and parsley blend in with floral greens, making a pretty addition to the garden that gives you great flavors for the kitchen, too. They can be grown indoors easily, or planted in a pot that can go indoors or out.

DRIED SPICES

BAY LEAVES

CARAWAY SEEDS

CARDAMOM

CHILI POWDER

CINNAMON

CLOVES (WHOLE)

CUMIN

CURRY POWDER

FENNEL SEEDS

GINGER

MUSTARD (DRY)

NUTMEG

OREGANO

PEPPER

SAFFRON

SALT

Spices, Oils and Vinegars

Having a laden rack of dried herbs and spices pleases cooks almost as much as, if not more than, a full shelf of assorted cookbooks. Curry and chili powders when matched with nonfat plain yogurt or sour cream make quick dips or sauces for guests. The other classics, such as bay leaves, cinnamon and cloves deserve a place in every cook's kitchen.

Look to the vinegars and oils for signs of a knowledgeable cook. Safflower or other polyunsaturated oil indicates someone who is health conscious or must lower his or her cholesterol. Oriental sesame oil, which the health-conscious food writer Marian Burros "can't be without," usually finds a home with pasta lovers; add 1 or 2 teaspoons to a finished dish, tossing just before serving. Walnut and other fragile nut oils point out a salad aficionado in most cases, and olive oil indicates a lover of rich tastes—the darker the oil, the more pungent. Extra virgin olive oil is the most flavorful, "pure" or "fine," the least. Whatever the variety, olive oil is a monosaturate, which means that it too is okay to use if someone is watching his or her cholesterol intake. Paired with a fragrant, wine-based balsamic vinegar and a dollop of Dijon mustard, olive oil produces an all-purpose salad dressing or vinaigrette. (Store it in the refrigerator to retain its freshness; the oil will be cloudy only until it warms up to room temperature again. Also refrigerate the sesame and fragile nut oils and use as soon as possible.)

White vinegar is handy to have around for cleaning as well as for eating. Mix a small amount with water in a glass pot to take away coffee stains; combine with baking soda to tackle heavy-duty grime on pots and pans. (Remember, entertaining doesn't end with serving the meal.) Cider vinegar when used with a light touch can counter sweetness in many sauces and combinations; a little in cole slaw perks up the mayonnaise; and you can even use it diluted as a last-resort basting sauce for roast chicken if you have nothing better.

OILS AND VINEGARS

OLIVE OIL

SAFFLOWER OIL

WALNUT OIL

BALSAMIC VINEGAR

CIDER VINEGAR

HERB VINEGARS

RED WINE VINEGAR

WHITE VINEGAR

FRIDGE STAPLES

BUTTER OR MARGARINE

CARROTS

CELERY

CHUTNEY

CREAM CHEESE

EGGS

LEMONS

LIMES

MILK

ONIONS

ORANGE JUICE

PARMESAN CHEESE

Freezer and Refrigerator Staples

The staples for the refrigerator will need more monitoring than the pantry staples. The foods spoil more quickly and because of their proximity to hungry hands may disappear more quickly too.

Tracy Kelley, the owner of Great Performances caterers in New York City, and Marian Burros, who writes about food for the *New York Times,* both stress the importance of keeping nonfat or lowfat yogurt in the refrigerator, a trend that reflects the growing awareness of the need to eat healthy food. You can use it on steamed vegetables and potatoes, in blender drinks instead of fattier milk and as a base for some sauces.

Parmesan cheese perks up salads, pastas, meats and more. Grate it as you go, using an all-purpose grater or a small, hand-held Mouli grater. The chutney and salsa—which can be bought through the mail (see Sources, pages 138 to 139)—bring a tangy bite to impromptu meals prepared with pantry staples. Lemons are good during the cooking as well as the eating phases of a small party; squeeze a little lemon juice on green vegetables to flavor them and keep them from discoloring, add lemon slices to water or seltzer, stuff a chicken with lemon or use a slice or two for fish *en papillote.*

© Michael Grand

Although it's not on the list, I always try to have on hand at least one kind of green vegetable: broccoli, Brussels sprouts, green beans, spinach, zucchini. The spinach and zucchini are particularly practical since they can be used to stuff meats and fish, they complement eggs and they prove themselves worthy either hot or cold. As I mentioned before, with just a squeeze of lemon and a pat or two of butter, they sit well on a dinner plate with relatively no preparation.

Carrots and celery keep in the refrigerator for at least a week, especially if washed and placed in a glass or small pitcher of cold water. Paired with curry and yogurt or cottage cheese, these crunchy veggies provide an easy, healthy hors d'oeuvre; sliced thin and sautéed with fresh herbs and olive oil, they can take the place of a green vegetable; and if you pull the soup stock from the freezer, they enhancc a plain broth with or without pasta or rice.

Which brings us to soup stocks, indispensable staples if you plan to entertain often. I make the stocks while making another meal, killing two birds with one stone. If you poach a chicken or fish, save the poaching water. In many cases, with a quick straining and defatting, you've got stock. I tend to use chicken and vegetable stocks more frequently than beef stock. Vegetable stock is quite simple: just save your odd pieces of carrot (including tops), celery (including tops), broccoli, parsnips, onion (including skin) and garlic. Add a few spices —thyme, marjoram, bay leaves and peppercorns—and let it all cook for about two hours. Then strain the liquid. The stocks freeze well and you can use them as sauce bases, poaching water for a more flavorful end product, soups, pureeing liquids and for basting. Try freezing the stock in ice cube trays; once frozen, store the cubes in airtight plastic bags. You can use a cube or two easily for sauces and even make a quick cup of soup, as speedily as if you used a bouillon cube.

The orange juice can also pinch hit for basting, pureeing and saucing, in addition to helping out in the bar area.

© C Weil/FPG International

Freezer Staples

My list of freezer staples may be shorter than some because I live near a fish store and a butcher. However, these few essentials have made life much easier, especially after a hard day's work. In fact, you could prepare an impressive meal from what's in the freezer. Serve a butter flavored with chives, garlic, parsley or tarragon on a prime cut of beef for a simple main course. Complement it with a side of fresh linguine with pesto. Then finish off the meal with a berry tart (made from berries and pie crust) and homemade chocolate truffles. Ideally, you'd also serve a salad, but the essence of entertaining well is doing the best with what you've got.

FREEZER STAPLES

BERRIES

FLAVORED BUTTERS

FRESH PASTA

PESTO

PIE CRUST

SOUP STOCKS

TOMATO SAUCE

TRUFFLES

© Steven Mark Needham/Envision

Using A Caterer

Some people splurge on clothing; others take long, hot baths helped along by evocative scents and a good book or crossword puzzle. Still others allow young gentlemen or ladies—strangers, sometimes in odd dress—into their houses to take over their kitchens.

Caterers are rarely necessary for a small party, but if you want that splurge, that luxurious feeling of doing something nice for yourself, ask a caterer to help with your next party of 10 or 12. The option to choose a menu depends on the caterer; most professionals like to hear what you have in mind, then will come up with their own menu that incorporates your ideas with their specialties.

"Small parties usually cost more per person than large ones, given the same menu. In fact, the cost of a catered meal at home for fewer than 25 people approaches restaurant prices," writes Sarah Button in *Money* magazine. So, the idea behind hiring a caterer for a small party goes back to the game. It's a novelty. It's refreshing for you. It's a new tactic, a surprise move.

Tracey Kelley, owner of Great Performances caterers in New York, stresses that the two most important facts to relay to a caterer are what type of party you want—lunch, dinner, tea or whatever—and how many guests you plan to invite. Beyond that, everything is negotiable, or you can let the caterer plan the whole shebang. Because you're ultimately calling the shots, you can even—with most caterers—make a dish or two yourself, sharing the space with your hired hands.

Settle the menu ahead of time and, if the caterer is using your kitchen, find out when he plans to arrive and with how many people. Do you want servers or just preparers? Do you want them dressed a certain way? You'll probably want to call at least two caterers, so keep a list of questions and answers. The list may also help for parties you host at a later date. Check the contract for responsibilities: Who will clean up? Who will supply the food and drink? (Many caterers do not have a liquor license, so you'll be responsible for buying the beverages.) What happens if something breaks?

In terms of finance, tax and tip may not always be figured in the quoted price. Plan to pay as much as fifty percent of the total in advance, the rest due just before or after the party. And be forewarned, many caterers do not accept credit cards.

How do you find the caterer? The phone directory is a good place to start, but you might spend more time tasting samples than you'd planned. Or ask friends, colleagues, your company's party planner, even restaurateurs, whom they suggest.

TIPS FOR HIRING A CATERER

Before you hire, ask questions about price (does it include tax and tips?); deposits and cancellations; and be sure—absolutely sure—that you taste samples of their food. Here are some other suggestions that will help you hire the right caterer:

• Don't expect that the per-person price for a small party will be cheaper than that for a larger party. Much of the same work goes into both, so if anything, that cost will be higher. If you hire a caterer, it's for convenience, not for cost effectiveness.

• Know what you want for your party—or have as clear an idea as possible before you call the caterer. This includes asking about coffee urns and coat racks as well as hors d'oeuvres.

• Don't feel embarrassed about the equipment in your kitchen—and never tell them you have more than you do. An honest appraisal will help deter last-minute disasters when the caterer shows up ready to use your equipment to get the party rolling.

BAR STAPLES

BLENDED WHISKEY

BOURBON

COGNAC OR
BRANDY

GIN

RUM (DARK)

RUM (LIGHT)

SCOTCH

DRY SHERRY

SPIRITS

TEQUILA

VODKA

A WELL-STOCKED BAR

When the Unsinkable Molly Brown belts out "Belly up to the bar, boys," everyone understands that drinking means a roaring good time. And drinking usually means alcohol. Yet, what's appropriate at a party these days is different than it used to be. This is true at cocktail parties as well as sit-down dinners.

Who would know this better than the author of *The American Dictionary of Food and Drink,* John Mariani, who ranks among the "Who's Who of Cooking in America." Mariani writes, "Now, at a time when genteel traditions such as double-breasted suits and elegant dresses are being resurrected, the cocktail—an American institution if ever there was one—is making a comeback, both in restaurants and at home."

The days of the well-stocked bar are reappearing. Stress diversity and creativity rather than quantity. As with your food pantry, however, you must use common sense and stock what appeals to you and to the friends you entertain the most.

The liquors listed below represent the traditional choices for a full home bar. Not everyone enjoys the smack of tequila,

MIXERS

CLUB SODA OR
SELTZER

COLA

GINGER ALE

TONIC WATER

LIQUEURS

ALMOND-FLAVORED:
*AMARETTO DI
SARONNO,
GALLIANO*

BLACK
CURRANT–FLAVORED:
CREME DE CASSIS

CHERRY-FLAVORED:
CHERRY MARNIER

CHOCOLATE-FLAVORED:
*CREME DE CACAO,
MARIE BRIZARD
CHOCOLAT, SABRA
(WITH ORANGES),
VANDERMINT
(WITH MINT)*

COCONUT-FLAVORED:
*CREME DE
COCONUT, MALIBU*

COFFEE-FLAVORED:
KAHLUA, TIA MARIA

HERB-FLAVORED:
*BENEDICTINE, B&B,
CHARTREUSE*

though, or craves a cognac after a satisfying meal. Start with two or three bottles and experiment using fresh juices, bottles of liqueurs and mixers. Add bottles, one or two at a time, as you become familiar with the drinks they can produce.

If drinking is not a problem for any of your friends, plan a tasting party as you would for wine—only use one or two hard liquors at a time. Offer small amounts (half or quarter the normal portions) of four drinks, spacing each one out around a well-chosen appetizer. Plan the party for the afternoon or surprise everyone by asking them to a sleepover.

One of my favorite parties began quite by accident when I was still in high school. It was a hot day when a friend came by on his bike, thirsty from the ride. Two other bikers followed him into the backyard and within a few minutes another nearby pal walked over to see what was going on. I quickly assembled all the wet and tasty things I could find in the fridge: grape, grapefruit, orange and cranberry juices; apricot nectar, which my mother always kept around for our occasional sore throats; ginger ale, root beer, cream soda, and thanks to my dad, seltzer in an old-fashioned siphon bottle. We spread the beverage containers, many of which were partly finished, on the picnic table and proceeded to mix and match. What we didn't

© Michael Kingsford/Envision

drink, we used to water the roses—although some of our concoctions became remembered successes.

A nonalcoholic mix-and-match party becomes much more fun nowadays with flavored seltzer and the addition of fruit: watermelon, citrus fruits, peaches, pears, mangos and berries. Cream, yogurt and milk bring to mind Creamsicles and can inspire great combinations. If you kick in a blender, you may have to let everyone have

LIQUEURS
Continued

HONEY-FLAVORED:
*DRAMBUIE,
IRISH MIST*

LICORICE-FLAVORED:
*ANISETTE, OUZO,
PERNOD, SAMBUCA*

MINT-FLAVORED:
*CREME DE MENTHE,
RUMPLE MINZE,
SCHNAPPS*

ORANGE-FLAVORED:
*COINTREAU,
CURACAO, GRAND
MARNIER,
TRIPLE SEC*

RASPBERRY-FLAVORED:
*CREME DE
FRAMBOISE*

**ASSORTED
APERITIFS:**
*CAMPARI, LILLET,
DRY VERMOUTH,
SWEET VERMOUTH*

EXTRAS

ANGOSTURA
BITTERS

CINNAMON STICKS

COARSE SALT

FRESH LEMONS,
LIMES

FRESH MINT

GRENADINE

HEAVY CREAM

HORSERADISH

MILK

OLIVES
(PITTED, GREEN)

PEARL ONIONS

PEPPER

SUPERFINE SUGAR
(OR SIMPLE SYRUP)

TABASCO™

WHOLE CLOVES

© Michael Grand

a turn at being mix master. You can easily add alcohol to the list of raw ingredients; just watch your guests' consumption and stay relatively sober yourself.

When calculating how much to buy, keep in mind that if you're entertaining often, you might want to plan ahead and shop in quantity. Many liquor stores now offer mixed cases of wine. For a cocktail party, forget the name and plan on no more than two full drinks per person (especially for those who are driving). You can still pour four half-sized strong drinks or four full-sized weak ones. Wine drinkers usually sip about four partially filled glasses, too. Diners tend to be satisfied with a little less. I'm not a heavy drinker, nor do I like to see my guests stone drunk, but to each his own.

ELEGANT CHILLED WINE

For an elegant flair, freeze an empty wine bottle—the same size as the bottle you'll be serving—in a wax-coated milk carton not quite filled with water; the ice will freeze into a block. Fill the bottle with lukewarm—not hot—water and carefully inch the empty bottle out. Remove the milk carton mold and place a full bottle of wine in the center of the ice, and voila—you can keep your white wine chilled! Another pretty tip for anytime of the year but especially in summer: Freeze pansies or other edible blossoms in individual ice cubes and float them in a punch bowl or even in drinks if you replenish them in fresh glasses.

© Simon Feldman/Envision

JUICES

CRANBERRY

GRAPEFRUIT

LIME

ORANGE

PINEAPPLE

TOMATO

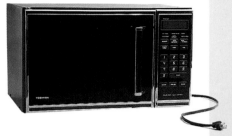

USING THE MICROWAVE

Here are some good tips for using your microwave to cook for a small party:

• Beginners should familiarize themselves with their microwave by first cooking vegetables, heating sauces and making risottos before attempting a main dish. Using a conventional oven in combination with a microwave should make it easier to time foods so they're ready when you want them to be.

• Don't assume you can automatically reduce or increase recipe amounts as you would with a standard recipe.

• Microwave with dishes—glass, plain ceramics and some earthenware—that are pretty enough to serve from.

• Add salt to dishes after they're out of the microwave, and in general, use spices sparingly. The microwave picks up flavors more readily than a standard oven. There are notable exceptions—garlic and cumin, for example—that require greater quantities than normal.

• Offer your guests heated finger towels after a meal involving finger food. Dampen thin, white washcloths with water and a few drops of lemon juice. Squeeze out the excess water, then heat the cloths in the microwave on high for approximately thirty seconds.

Gourmet to Go

An alternative to cooking and catering is ordering out. What once was considered taboo has now become quite chic, especially in cities. In fact, a recent issue of the *New York Times Magazine* said "Carryout has gone haute." Pizza and Chinese food are being eclipsed by more interesting offerings from gourmet delis, Indian res-

taurants and sushi bars. Even posh, pricey restaurants are playing the game. New York's Arcadia restaurant offers box lunches and dinners. For $30 per person and 24 hours advance notice, you can order a three-course meal centering around braised lamb shanks with orzo and ratatouille, for example. Or salmon. Or chicken in a pot.

Diners in Boston, Cambridge, Chicago,

Cleveland, Dallas, Houston, Los Angeles, San Francisco, and Washington can find restaurants or services eager to bend to this trend. To keep up with the growing competition some even deliver. If you live elsewhere or have a favorite restaurant that doesn't advertise carryout, they may still be willing to prepare a meal for you if you arrange it ahead of time and pick it up when the restaurant is not busy. This is just one more advantage of hosting a *small* party.

You might also consider *supplementing* a homemade meal with take-out or mail-order foods. A friend and I once put together a meal with three kinds of smoked hams (corncob-, mahogany-, and hickory-smoked), a variety of accompanying mustards, sourdough bread, wild rice with wild mushrooms, green salad with shallot vermouth vinaigrette and vanilla ice cream with fudge sauce and ginger crisps. The only foods that did *not* arrive at our doorsteps via the U.S. mail or U.P.S. were the lettuce and ice cream. (See Sources, pages 138 to 139 for addresses.)

Planning for a party and stocking the pantry should be combined. If you keep tabs on what you've got—including what you tend *not* to use—you can keep your kitchen stocked with what become your own personal essential items. So when it's time for a party, shopping becomes easier; you'll

have a better idea of what you want and, most likely, won't need to shop for as much. And, of course, you'll have the flexibility to entertain at a moment's notice. The planned party has its place but so does inviting a few friends home after work or finding out it's someone's birthday and asking him or her over the next day even though you don't have time to plan a party.

Although sophisticated take-out meals with crystal stemware and cloth napkins have appeared in the marketplace, traditional Chinese food still sets the standard. Either way, takeout is an easy alternative to a home-cooked meal.

THE PARTY'S OVER

Taking in the sight of a small kitchen piled high with dirty plates and leftover food, a friend once remarked to me, "You must *love* to entertain, because I know you don't like to clean up." I was on my own, dealing with a mess that took almost two hours to get through. Thank goodness I've learned since then. *The easiest way to clean up after a meal is to clean up before the meal.* If it means adding an extra fifteen minutes or half hour to your pre-party schedule, by all means, add the time in. It's well worth it.

Just as a good cook organizes the ingredients before preparing a recipe, a good host cleans up as he or she goes along. Put ingredients away immediately after you finish the portion of the recipe that calls for them. Wipe the counter before starting on the next phase. Wash the dishes as the food cooks, making sure you've left ample space for dishes that are drying.

If your kitchen is small and you have a dishwasher, here's a tip for those few utensils you may need to re-use. Start with an empty dishwasher. When I'm cooking I know that I won't use glasses and rarely will I use small pieces of cookware that can't fit on the bottom rack, so I leave the top rack empty even while I fill the bottom with dirty dishes. When you hand-wash your frequently used items such as measuring cups and colander, use the top rack as a drying space for just-washed dishes. Without a dishwasher, use a specific corner of the drying rack for dishes that will be used again.

I usually take out the garbage and give the counters a final wipe-down before guests arrive. That way, too, I have the option of setting out dessert plates or coffee cups or whatever to help the flow of the meal.

Then, once the meal is over, your kitchen is still clean enough for you to ask friends to help clear the table, if you prefer their help—and clean enough for guests not to feel guilty leaving you alone with a mess.

Here's an idea that will help you organize your cleanup, and will help keep the environment clean. If you don't recycle, take a cue from those who do. Set up separate bags prior to the party; one for returnable bottles and cans, one for paper and one for all else (or whatever you can recycle locally). Not only will you be able to return the bottles and cans, but you'll also be sending signals to your guests to be neat if they help you clean up.

If your guests spill a little more than you expected and you're worried about some stains at the end of the party, perhaps these two cleanup tips will help. Try shaving cream, regular (not gel) toothpaste, salt or club soda when you come across a stubborn carpet stain. Dab a little of one of the above "cleaners" on your carpet, let it sit for two or three minutes and then blot or vacuum the spot when it is dry. (Be sure to test an out-of-view piece of your carpet first, to make sure the color won't fade.)

On older, dark wood furniture that has a buildup of old wax, try removing water spots by ironing them (again, test a small area first). Place a smooth dish towel on the table and run an iron over the spot at low temperature. The whitish gray rings should disappear.

OUTDOOR PARTIES

Eating outside is a pleasure. Senses appear heightened by the air, whether it is crisped and cool or warm and languid. Outdoor smells further accentuate the flavors of your meal, and memories become more potent, or so it seems. Moving a party out of doors really does not pose a problem once you've thought through your game plan. You've got to consider lighting, seating and serving foremost. And back up any plans with an indoor alternative. For tips on lighting, see page 22.

Seating need not be that different from an indoor buffet. You can provide a table and chairs; a tablecloth for a traditional picnic; or a low table and giant pillows on top of a cleaned dhurrie or Oriental rug.

Winds—or the potential for winds—calls for advance planning. Napkins held down by a geode or other interesting mineral work as a striking table addition. Bring the food out as it will be served. All last-minute preparation belongs in the kitchen. You don't want to have empty containers blowing around outside.

For all but the most elegant parties, station a garbage bag outside in a spot that's away from the food table.

The two parties outlined below show that outdoor parties are not limited to on-the-ground picnics, or to balmy summer months. Even in winter, a good picnic with piping hot chili and warmed dessert can make an everlasting impression.

MENU

FOR 5

FIVE ALARM CHILI

CRUSTY FRENCH
BREAD

HONEY GRILLED
CHICKEN

BREAD PUDDING
WITH APRICOT
GLAZE

WINTER PICNIC

Date: January 19, 1840
Occasion: Discovery of Antarctica

The "pepper" we call chili is not a pepper at all. The misnomer dates back to Columbus's day, when he—or one of his contemporaries—thought the spicy *capsicum*, or chili, plants of the New World were relatives of the East Indian *Piper nigrum* we call black pepper. An easy mistake to make, considering Columbus thought he was in India. But chili does share the same genus with green and red bell peppers.

If you think that a jalapeño—one of the many kinds of chili peppers—is tongue-tingling hot, keep in mind that the lowly jalapeño rates only a 15 out of a possible 120 on a professional's scale of hotness. When choosing peppers, the best strategy is to ask someone in the know.

Upstairs, Downstairs Catering of Madison, Wisconsin, prepares a chili recipe that may knock your socks off. To cool it down, mix in fewer crushed chilies. Otherwise, you'll be depending on the not-so-reliable partnership of sour cream and bread to put out the fire. On the other hand, this piquant chili will, if not keep you hot, at least keep you from thinking about the cold.

For a proper picnic, take to the outdoors. Pack the chili in a family-size insulated container; grill the chicken over a barbecue (provided you have one); and keep the bread pudding warm by packing it between two layers of cardboard covered with aluminum foil. The ideal winter picnic calls for, of all things, a party pooper—someone who's not so keen on hiking, skating, skiing or whatever else that's keeping you outdoors. Prepare and pack everything in advance except for the pudding. Once the pudding's in the loaf pan, it just needs to be baked and packed, a simple job for the party pooper.

Top off the meal with thermoses of hot coffee or tea and hot chocolate. Bring along some heavy cream and a rotary beater for a fresh whipped crown for the cocoa.

This chili and chicken menu works just as well inside, and you can preserve the picnic feeling. Broil the chicken instead of grilling it; and rather than dining at the table, set the "table" on a well-cushioned, warm floor. Move the furniture to create a picnic area indoors. Put the dhurrie rug down, light a few candles, serve the food family style and voila!

You don't need to hold your winter picnic in as foreboding a location as this—deepest Antarctica. Find a good picnic table in the snow, or a shelter. And if that idea is still too cold for you, move your "picnic" to a well-carpeted floor inside.

FIVE ALARM CHILI

½ pound ground Italian sausage

¼ pound ground beef

1 onion, chopped finely

1 stalk celery, chopped

19 ounce can kidney beans, drained

¼ cup dark beer

1 cup tomato juice

¼ cup tomato paste

⅔ cup chopped fresh tomatoes

3 to 4 tablespoons chili powder

2 tablespoons chopped parsley

1½ teaspoons sugar (optional)

1 teaspoon Tabasco™

½ tablespoon garlic powder

½ to 1 teaspoon cumin

1 teaspoon dried crushed chili peppers (optional)

½ teaspoon freshly ground black pepper

1 bay leaf

3 cups cooked rice

Salt to taste

Aged Wisconsin Cheddar cheese for garnish

½ pint sour cream

Sauté the Italian sausage, ground beef, onion and chopped celery until the beef is cooked. Drain off the fat and transfer the defatted ingredients to a saucepan. Add the beans, beer, tomato juice, tomato paste, fresh tomatoes and stir. Add the chili powder, parsley, sugar, Tabasco™ sauce, garlic powder, cumin, chili peppers, black pepper, bay leaf and salt; mix well. Simmer on low heat for approximately 30 minutes.

Serve over rice, if you like, with grated cheddar cheese and dollops of sour cream for garnish. (You may also want to set out an extra bowl of chopped onions for people who can't get enough.)

HONEY GRILLED CHICKEN

5 six-ounce chicken breasts

½ cup lemon juice

1 teaspoon ground ginger

4 tablespoons butter

¾ cups honey

2 tablespoons Dijon mustard

1 tablespoon White Wine Worcestershire Sauce

1½ teaspoons pre-mixed barbecue spice (optional)

¾ teaspoon garlic powder

2 tablespoons parsley (optional)

Wash the chicken breasts and pull the skin from them. Place them in a shallow pan or bowl for marinating. In a separate bowl or measuring cup, mix together the lemon juice and ginger; pour evenly over the chicken breasts. Marinate refrigerated for 4 hours, turning the chicken once after 2 hours.

After the chicken has marinated, make the grilling sauce. Melt 2 tablespoons of the butter over low heat with the honey, mustard, Worcestershire Sauce, barbecue spice (if you choose to use it), garlic powder and parsley (if used). Mix well and remove from the heat. Set aside.

Sauté the chicken breasts in the remaining butter for 5 minutes on each side. Using tongs, remove the breasts from the sauté pan and dip each piece in the honey-mustard sauce. Coat each piece well, and place on the broiler pan (or on a platter to take out to the barbecue). Grill for 1 to 2 minutes on each side, turning the chicken more often if necessary—watching to make sure that the honey sauce doesn't burn.

BREAD PUDDING

Approximately 1 loaf of white bread

¼ cup melted butter

¼ cup brown sugar

1 teaspoon cinnamon

½ cup raisins

¾ cup powdered milk

2½ cups boiling water

3 eggs

3 tablespoons sugar

1¼ teaspoons vanilla

Pinch of salt

Preheat oven to 350°.

Coat a loaf pan with nonstick spray. Heap the pan with chunks of white bread. Top with the melted butter, brown sugar, cinnamon and raisins.

Beat together the eggs, sugar, vanilla and salt until well mixed. Combine the powdered milk and boiling water; mix well; and add slowly to the egg-and-sugar mixture. Pour the batter into the loaf pan and cover with foil. Bake 45 to 60 minutes in a water bath. When done, the pudding should look solid, with no liquid, but not brown.

Apricot glaze

Juice of half an orange

½ tablespoon apricot brandy

½ cup apricot preserves

Mix together all the ingredients and serve over the warm bread pudding.

© Steven Mark Needham/Envision

MENU

FOR 4

MINTED
CUCUMBER
SALAD

LOBSTER SALAD
WITH PASSION
FRUIT SAUCE

BANANA
GONDOLAS

© Allan Weitz

BOAT PICNIC

Date: August 26, 1819
Occasion: Sea serpent sighting

The details will forever be lost, but one ordinary day in 1819 the Navy's Cheever Felch reported he saw a huge sea serpent. His claim is just one of numerous "sightings" of serpents from Loch Ness, Lake Champlain and all the oceans of the world.

These tales can help create an atmosphere of mystery and illusion. Add some dry ice, available at many ice-cream outlets, to simulate the smoke of a witch's brew. Because this is a picnic, each guest will help himself or herself to silverware, plates and napkins. Arrange for each person to pick from a grab bag before dinner as well. Inside the bag put a toy sea serpent, a crystal, a key and one other object—anything—that appeals to you. Wrap each well to disguise its shape. As dinner winds down, inform each guest that a mystery occurred on this boat, but no one knows what happened. Unwrap the object you picked from the grab bag and begin to tell a story based on the boat and the object. After you've established the time, place and main character of the story, at least, have one of your guests continue the tale. He or she must incorporate their object into the story.

Pack a Ouija board, tarot cards or runes to fill out the night if the storytelling grows cold. Or bring along a volume of sea tales or ghost stories and take turns reading out loud.

The meal is light, just enough to satisfy a laid-back crew. If your boat doesn't have a burner to heat the banana gondolas, just serve ice cream (you can keep it cold with dry ice, but be careful not to touch the dry ice; it can burn your skin). Spoon the apple-raisin-rum mixture, without the vanilla stick and bananas, over the ice cream.

The lobster salad and banana gondolas come straight from the seashore, from a Caribbean resort skilled at creating fantasies, L'Habitation in French St. Martin.

A trip to the local library, historical society or used bookstore may uncover wonderful old prints that can be bought (or photocopied and hand-colored) and used for place-mats, backdrops or invitations. This sea serpent is certain to liven up a party.

MINTED CUCUMBER SALAD

1 European seedless
cucumber

¼ cup mint

1 cup plain yogurt

Pinch of cumin

With a vegetable peeler, peel stripes down the cucumber, so some of the skin remains. Slice the cucumber thinly and set aside. Rinse the mint, then cut the leaves into thin strips across the length of the leaf. In a medium bowl, mix the yogurt and cumin. Add the mint, combining well. Then add the cucumbers, making sure all the slices are well coated. Refrigerate, covered, for approximately 2 hours.

© Grant Heilman

LOBSTER SALAD WITH PASSION FRUIT SAUCE

4 lobsters	1 teaspoon parsley
1/3 cup lobster cooking water	Lettuce or endive
1/3 cup passion fruit juice	1 tablespoon chervil (or parsley, if chervil is unavailable)
1/3 cup olive oil	
1 teaspoon basil	1 ripe mango

Steam the lobsters until done, about 8 minutes. Let them cool slightly, remove the lobster meat from the shell and chop it.

Prepare a sauce by combining the lobster cooking water, passion fruit juice and olive oil. Season the sauce with the basil and parsley.

Toss the lobster in the sauce and arrange it either on crisp lettuce or endive. Chop the chervil and sprinkle it over the salad. Peel and julienne the mango and garnish each plate with the fruit strips before serving.

BANANA GONDOLAS

2 tart apples, peeled and cored	2 tablespoons apricot jam
1/4 cup raisins	4 bananas
2 tablespoons light rum	1 vanilla stick

Preheat the oven to 375°.

Bake the apples in a buttered dish until soft, about 30 minutes. Soak the raisins in the rum for 2 to 3 minutes until they are somewhat plump. Drain the raisins, reserving the rum, then set them aside. Puree the apples in a food processor with the rum and the apricot jam. Set aside.

Make gondolas from aluminum foil using a banana's length of foil for each container. Fold the foil in half lengthwise, then crimp each end. As you crimp the foil, it should fall into a natural gondola-like shape. Peel the bananas and put one inside each gondola. Break the vanilla stick into fourths and lay a piece inside each gondola. Top each banana with equal amounts of the apple puree. Sprinkle each with raisins.

Close the gondolas and steam them for 10 to 15 minutes.

COCKTAIL PARTIES

No one knows for sure how the cocktail came by its name. Stories abound with such diversity as to include in their cast of characters a tavern owner during the American Revolution who kept a rooster's tail feathers in a glass on the bar and a New Orleans apothecary who measured his drinks with an egg cup, or *coquetier* in French.

However it came to be named, the cocktail has gained a new cachet. Food magazines intermittently publish cool drink recipes from hot restaurants, and their appeal is not limited solely to a cocktail party.

What then is a cocktail party? What immediately comes to mind is a stand-up affair with a variety of hors d'oeuvres. Food and presentation rather than beverage become the focal point.

The cocktail party scaled down to a small gathering has many of the same advantages as a sit-down dinner; with no more than a dozen people, the conversation flows easily and all of your guests should get to know each other. If your guests are game, play with them a bit, drawing on the novelty of the situation. Just as some theater has begun to rove from room to room, so can your party. Plan a moveable feast, literally, with tidbits served in assorted indoor and outdoor locations. Buy a mystery party game or invent your own. Plan a scavenger hunt where the clues are hidden with the next hors d'oeuvres.

MENU

FOR 10

JUMBO SHRIMP
WITH CLASSIC
COCKTAIL SAUCE

SMOKED SALMON
TRIANGLES

CAVIAR CUPS

PARMA PAPAYA

CRABCAKES WITH
REMOULADE
SAUCE

SCUBA POOL SPLASH

Date: June 1943
Occasion: Jacques Cousteau and Emile Gagnan introduced self-contained underwater breathing apparatus, or SCUBA.

Ever wanted to get underwater with the fish but were a little hesitant? Try the pool first. With a little help from a nearby scuba store or dive shop, you can splash into a pool geared up and ready to take on a barracuda or a shark—but the only other animals in the pool will be your friends.

A scuba pool splash, the brainchild of Marian Rivman, the spokesperson for the scuba equipment industry, gets people into the water and simulates a mini-dive under the care of a trained instructor. What Marian can do, you can do.

Ask your dive contact how much it will cost to provide rental equipment, pool time (if they book it) and an instructor to guide you through a splash party for ten people. Not everyone's going in the pool at once, so figure you'll need equipment for two or three people—that's also a good number for the divemaster to keep his eye on. (If your budget won't cover equipment rental, go ahead and have a party without the scuba diving—you'll still have fun.)

Invite your friends with a mounted cutout of the most colorful fish you can find in print. Be sure to request that guests bring bathing suits, fins, snorkels and masks if they have them, and good attitudes.

Present the food on new washed or napkin-lined fins as serving trays. Pass the tidbits around yourself; perhaps enlist a dive buddy to help. Tracy Kelly of Great Performances caterers in New York City developed the menu for this bash. She recommends a number of drinks to accompany the food, which you can have set up at different drink stations, modeling the decor to fit the name of the beverage: Try serving The Deep, a punch of sparkling wine and cranberry juice; Waterlilies, sparkling wine and orange juice; Coral Reefs, white wine with a dash of cassis; Regulators, white wine spritzers; and Wet Suits, glasses of chilled white wine.

If you can arrange to have a VCR set up in an anteroom near the pool, don't show *Jaws* but do try to play a Jacques Cousteau or National Geographic video continuously. Music can range from the Beach Boys to the Paul Winter Consort's whale sound albums.

Movie Still Archives

Though it was designed for serious research, you can use Jacques Cousteau's SCUBA gear to entertain your guests at an unusual party. If such extravagance isn't within your budget, substitute snorkeling equipment and diving props and gather around the pool for a good time.

© Stock Imagery

JUMBO SHRIMP WITH CLASSIC COCKTAIL SAUCE

1½ pounds jumbo shrimp, peeled and deveined

1 cup ketchup

2 tablespoons horseradish

Allow 3 shrimp per guest.

Bring a large pot of water to a boil. Add shrimp and cook just until pink, 2 to 3 minutes. Do not overcook. Drain the shrimp and immerse them in cold water to cool. Drain again and refrigerate.

For the cocktail sauce, mix ketchup and horseradish together and pour into a glass bowl approximately 4 inches in diameter. Arrange the shrimp on a tray with the bowl of sauces in the center and serve.

SMOKED SALMON TRIANGLES

¼ pound butter, softened

⅛ cup chopped chives

10 slices thinly sliced black bread

1 3- to 4-pound side of salmon, boned and skinned

1 bunch dill for garnish

Allow 3 to 4 pieces per guest.

Cream butter and chives together. Spread each slice of bread with a very thin layer of chive butter. Slice the salmon very thinly and arrange salmon slices to fit each slice of bread. Cut each slice of bread into triangles by slicing both diagonals. Garnish each triangle with a sprig of dill. Arrange on a flipper and serve.

CAVIAR CUPS

30 small bibb lettuce leaves (2 to 3 heads), washed and dried

½ pint sour cream or plain nonfat yogurt

3 tablespoons American malossol caviar

¼ cup chopped chives

Allow 3 pieces per guest.

Wash and dry the smaller (two-bite size) inner leaves of lettuce. Fill each leaf with a teaspoon of sour cream or plain nonfat yogurt (as a reduced fat alternative).

For an elegant look, put the sour cream or yogurt into a pastry bag and pipe it onto the lettuce leaves. Top the sour cream with approximately ¼ teaspoon of caviar, then sprinkle this with chopped chives.

PARMA PAPAYA

½ pound Parma ham, very
thinly sliced

30 wooden skewers

1 ripe papaya

Allow 3 pieces per guest.

Cut each slice of Parma ham lengthwise into 3 strips. Cut the papaya in half lengthwise and scoop out seeds carefully. Cut the papaya into quarters and cut each section again into quarters. Using a sharp paring knife, remove the skin from each wedge. Cut each wedge into bite-size pieces about 1 ½ inches long and ¾ inch wide. Wrap one strip of parma ham around each piece of papaya and skewer. Arrange on a flipper and serve immediately.

© G. French/FPG International

CRABCAKES WITH REMOULADE SAUCE

1 pound crabmeat picked clean, preferably fresh, not canned

2 cups bechamel sauce

1 bunch scallions, finely chopped

Salt to taste

Pepper to taste

Cayenne pepper to taste

1 cup plain bread crumbs

1 cup yellow cornmeal

2 tablespoons butter

Combine the picked crabmeat and warm bechamel sauce. Add the scallions and mix until evenly blended. Using the salt, pepper and cayenne, season to taste.

In another bowl, mix the breadcrumbs with the cornmeal. With two teaspoons, one in each hand, scoop out 32 equal-sized balls of the crab mixture. Using water to keep your hands moist, form each crab ball into cakes and bread each one with the crumb-and-cornmeal mixture.

Heat the butter in a heavy-bottomed sauté pan until almost brown. Sauté the crabcakes for approximately 1 minute on each side, six at a time. Cool briefly on a rack and serve warm with remoulade sauce.

Remoulade sauce

¼ cup capers, chopped	Cayenne pepper to taste
¼ cup cornichons, chopped	1 cup mayonnaise
1 shallot, finely chopped	1 cup sour cream
Salt to taste	Splash of dry white wine
Pepper to taste	2 tablespoons of chopped parsley

Combine ingredients in a large mixing bowl. Let the seasonings set for 3 to 4 hours before serving.

Yields 2 cups.

© Felicia Martinez/PhotoEdit

Bechamel sauce

¼ pound butter	1 bay leaf
½ cup flour	1 pinch nutmeg
1½ cups milk	Salt to taste
1 shallot, finely chopped	Pepper to taste

Melt the butter in a saucepan. Gradually whisk in the flour until the mixture reaches a smooth, pastelike consistency. Cook, stirring, over medium-low heat for another minute or two. Remove from the heat and set aside.

Heat the milk with the shallot, bay leaf, nutmeg, salt and pepper. Bring to a low boil, then whip in the roux (flour-butter mixture) gradually. Cook until thickened. When finished, pour the hot sauce into a bowl through a strainer to remove lumps. Let cool slightly before using or refrigerating.

Yields 2 cups.

MENU

FOR 10 TO 12

SMOKED TROUT
ON
PUMPERNICKEL

NEW POTATOES
WITH SOUR
CREAM AND
CAVIAR

CUCUMBER AND
CRAB CANAPES

MUSSELS
RAVIGOTE

FILLET

CHEESE BOARD

RUM CHOCOLATE
MOUSSE

EXOTIC COFFEES

BLACKOUT PARTY

Date: November 9, 1965
Occasion: Great blackout

Send out an invitation on black paper with silver ink; punch a hole in one corner and with black-and-white ribbon attach a black mini-flashlight; and ask your friends to dress in black and white.

Your party excuse—the great blackout that stretched from Canada through New England and New York—gives the first kick to party conversation. Where were you when the blackout struck? If where you live was unaffected, pick another dark day, a day of a hurricane or tornado when lights went out and you had to rely on a gas stove, fireplace or barbecue.

Dim the lights inside. Use votive candles in glass for the best effect and the least mess. If you've got a fireplace, light a fire and stock an evening's supply of firewood inside so you don't have to interrupt the party. Arrange for guests to sit on pillows, chairs or a sofa in front of the fire or go outdoors and build a bonfire if you can.

It's the perfect night to play a game of Sardines. Do you remember that one?

One person hides in a place where others can join him. As the hunters find the hider, one by one they become hiders, pressing in with the original hider. By the end of the game, you'll have all of your guests but one hiding together in a tight squeeze and one person searching.

Sardines can split the evening up. Pass around the new potatoes, smoked trout, mussels and crab before playing. The fillet and dessert and coffee follow. And for a nightcap, try Pernod or another anisette that turns white when water is added to it.

Use black paper plates that can go directly into the fireplace after they've been scraped (be sure not to use wax-coated plates). Set up a small, unobtrusive black-bag-covered wastebasket near the fireplace, and delegate the responsibility to one friend to help clean up.

Thanks to Shamus Butler, a graduate of the Culinary Institute of America, these recipes are easy to prepare.

POWER FAILURE SNARLS NORTHEAST; 800,000 ARE CAUGHT IN SUBWAYS HERE; AUTOS TIED UP, CITY GROPES IN DARK

Snarl at Rush Hour Spreads Into 9 States

10,000 in the National Guard and 5,000 Off-Duty Policemen Are Called to Service in New York

By PETER KIHSS

The largest power failure in history blacked out nearly all of New York City, parts of nine Northeastern states and two provinces of southeastern Canada last night. Some 80,000 square miles, in which perhaps 25 million people live and work, were affected.

It was more than three hours before the first lights came back on in any part of the New York City area. When they came on in Nassau and Suffolk Counties at 9 P.M., overloads plunged the area into darkness again in 10 minutes.

Striking at the evening rush hour, the power failure trapped 800,000 riders on New York City's subways. Railroads halted. Traffic was jammed. Airplanes found themselves circling, unable to land. But the Defense Department reported that the Strategic Air Command and other defense installations functioned without a halt.

National Guard Called Out

Five thousand off-duty policemen were summoned to duty here. Ten thousand National Guardsmen were called up in New York City alone. Other militiamen were alerted in Rhode Island and Massachusetts, as well as upstate New York.

The lights and the power went out first at 5:17 P.M. somewhere along the Niagara frontier of New York state. Nobody could tell why for hours afterward.

The tripping of automatic switches hurtled the blackout eastward across the state—to Buffalo, Rochester, Syracuse, Utica, Schnectady, Troy and Albany.

Within four minutes the line of darkness had plunged across Massachusetts all the way to Boston. It was like a pattern of falling dominoes—darkness sped southward through Connecticut, northward into Vermont, New Hampshire, Maine and Canada.

Sputtering at 5:27

At 5:27 P.M. the lights began sputtering in New York City, and within seconds the giant Consolidated Edison system blacked out in Manhattan, the Bronx, Queens and most of Brooklyn—but not in Staten Island and parts of Brooklyn that were interconnected with the Public Service Electric and Gas Company of New Jersey.

The darkness probed outward into northern New Jersey, up into Westchester and Rockland Counties, eastward into Long Island.

As far south as Washington, a Potomac Electric Power Company spokesman reported a power "dip" at 5:30 P.M., lasting less than a minute and virtually unnoticed in the nation's capital.

In Pennsylvania, the blackout spread through Pittsburgh and Reading into parts of Philadelphia and then into New Jersey along the coast above Atlantic City.

President Johnson, in Austin, Tex., ordered the full resources of the Federal Government thrown into an investigation by the Federal Power Commission. The Federal Bureau of Investigation, the Defense Department and other agencies were ordered to report "at the earliest possible moment."

The anniversary of the great blackout of 1965 offers a wonderful opportunity to have a few friends over. Just be sure to ask your guests to dress in black and white, flashlights allowed.

SMOKED TROUT ON PUMPERNICKEL

1 loaf pumpernickel bread, sliced (approximately 10 slices)

1/2 pound smoked trout (approximately half a trout)

1 pound cream cheese

30 large capers

Remove the crusts from the pumpernickel. Cut into 3 finger strips. Set aside.

Fill a pastry bag with the cream cheese. Pipe a ribbon of cream cheese down the center of each finger of bread.

Cut the trout into pieces just smaller than the bread fingers, and arrange one piece of trout on top of each piece of bread. Pipe a small rosette of cream cheese in the center of each piece of trout. Place a caper on the cream cheese rosette. Using a toothpick, open the outer leaves of the caper to resemble a flower bud.

NEW POTATOES WITH SOUR CREAM AND CAVIAR

15 to 20 egg-size red bliss potatoes

1/2 tablespoon salt

2 cups sour cream

1 ounce black caviar (lumpfish or beluga)

Peel the potatoes and ladle them into a pot of salted boiling water. Cook about 15 to 20 minutes, until tender. Drain the potatoes, then shock them in cold water (to prevent them from cooking any longer). Slice the potatoes in half horizontally; slice a portion off the bottom of each half so they can stand on their own; and scoop out the center with a melon baller or small spoon.

Fill a pastry bag with the sour cream, and using a small star tip, pipe a generous amount of the sour cream into each potato half. The sour cream should stand approximately 1/4- to 1/2-inch above the potato.

Garnish each with caviar. Chill until ready to serve.

© Gordon E. Smith

CUCUMBER AND CRAB CANAPES

1 large European seedless
cucumber

1 1/2 pounds of cooked snow
crab meat

4 to 6 tablespoons
mayonnaise

Salt to taste

Pepper to taste

Cayenne pepper to taste

15 black olives

Peel 4 stripes down the length of the cucumber so the peeled stripes alternate with the skin stripes. Slice the cucumber into rounds about 1/4-inch thick. A large cucumber should yield approximately 30 slices. Arrange on a platter.

Pick through the crabmeat, making sure no shell remains in the meat. Squeeze any excess water from the meat. In a food processor, puree the crabmeat until fine (using the stop-and-go button). Add the mayonnaise to bind the pureed crabmeat. Transfer the crabmeat from the processor to a bowl and stir in salt, pepper and cayenne. Fill a pastry bag with the crabmeat puree, and using a #5 star tip, pipe the mixture onto each round of cucumber. Top each round with a thin slice of black olive.

MUSSELS RAVIGOTE

Approximately 30 to 40 fresh
mussels

2 cups dry white wine

2 bay leaves

4 cloves

Rinse the mussels, scrubbing well. Remove the beards and set aside.

In a heavy skillet bring the wine, bay leaves and cloves to a boil. Reduce the heat to a simmer immediately, add the mussels and cover. Continue to simmer 5 to 10 minutes, until the shells have opened. (Discard any that are still shut.)

Drain the mussels and remove the top shells. Let cool. Arrange on a platter and serve with the Ravigote Sauce.

Ravigote sauce

1 teaspoon Dijon mustard

3 teaspoons red wine vinegar

4 tablespoons olive oil

1 teaspoon tarragon, chopped

1 hard-boiled egg, finely
chopped

1½ tablespoons fresh chervil,
chopped (substitute more
parsley if you can't find chervil)

1½ tablespoons parsley, finely
chopped

Salt to taste

Pepper to taste

In a nonreactive bowl, whisk together the mustard and vinegar. Slowly add the olive oil, whisking continuously until the mixture becomes thick. Stir in the remaining ingredients.

Spoon over the mussels. Cover and refrigerate until ready to serve.

© Greg Kopacka/Stock Imagery

FILLET

5 to 7 tablespoons black peppercorns	6 cloves garlic
2 to 4 tablespoons oil	Salt to taste
	Pepper to taste
1 tenderloin of beef (2 to 3 pounds)	1 pound butter, softened
Paprika to taste	2 loaves fresh French bread

Two hours prior to the party, season the tenderloin. First, crack the peppercorns. Put the peppercorns in a wooden bowl and cover with a clean, smooth dish towel. Steadying the bowl with one hand, crack the peppercorns with a mallet. Alternatively, grind the peppercorns coarsely or use a mortar and pestle.

Using your hands, rub the oil on the fillet. Sprinkle generously with the paprika. Pat the fillet in the pepper until the meat is well covered on both sides.

In the oven broiler or on an open barbecue, sear the meat well on both sides to give the fillet a dark exterior. Continue cooking until center of fillet is done to your taste. Remove the meat to a carving board or platter and let stand for 10 minutes before carving.

While the meat is cooking, prepare the garlic croutons. Mince the garlic and add it and the salt and pepper to the softened butter, creaming to mix. Cut the French bread into slices on the diagonal. Spread the garlic butter on each slice. Lightly toast the slices on a sheet pan under the broiler or directly on the grill, about 2 to 3 minutes. Watch closely. Reassemble the croutons in the shape of the original loaf and wrap the bread in foil.

While the meat is standing, reheat the foil-wrapped bread. Slice the fillet and serve over croutons.

© Tony Generico/FPG International

CHEESE BOARD

A variety of cheeses is always a welcome addition to any cocktail party. Try designing a presentation of a number of different cheeses and fruit. A delicatessan will be able to supply you with a good combination of white cheeses, such as French Brie, Boursin au Poivre, Tomme au Raisin, Gorgonzola or Roquefort, Montrachet Ash and Black Rind Wisconsin Cheddar. These will be striking when presented along with dark purple grapes and black figs. The contrasting tastes and colors will entice your guests.

© Steven Mark Needham/Envision

RUM CHOCOLATE MOUSSE

8 tablespoons sugar

4 tablespoons rum

7 ounces of semi-sweet chocolate

2½ cups plus 3 tablespoons heavy cream

3 egg whites

1 teaspoon vanilla

Chocolate shavings for garnish (optional)

Combine 6 tablespoons of the sugar with the rum in a saucepan over low heat for a few minutes until dissolved. Set aside.

Melt the chocolate and 3 tablespoons of the heavy cream in a double boiler. Stir in the rum and sugar. In a separate bowl, beat the egg whites until stiff. In another bowl, whip 1½ cups of the heavy cream. When the chocolate-rum mixture is almost cool (approximately 90° to 100° on a candy thermometer), gently fold in the egg whites. Then gently fold in the whipped cream.

Place the mousse immediately in long-stemmed serving glasses. Cover with plastic wrap and refrigerate for at least 2 hours.

Just prior to serving, whip 1 cup of the heavy cream, gradually adding 2 tablespoons of sugar and the vanilla. Top each serving of mousse with a generous dollop of whipped cream. Garnish with shaved chocolate.

EXOTIC COFFEES

Serve a selection of coffee drinks to complement the dessert. Simply add 1 to 1 ½ ounces of your favorite liqueur or cordial to each cup of freshly brewed coffee. Some popular choices are:

Irish Coffee made with Irish whiskey

Venetian Coffee made with brandy

Roman Coffee made with anisette

Monk's Coffee made with Frangelico

Mexican Coffee made with Kahlua

Coffee d'Amore made with Amaretto

Jamaican Coffee made with Tia Maria

Top each cup of coffee with a heaping spoonful of whipped cream and garnish with a coffee bean, chocolate shavings or freshly grated nutmeg.

TASTING PARTIES

When you fall in love with food and begin opening your eyes to the diversity of treats around, you notice blood oranges, star fruit, squid-ink pasta and christophene. Although the stores identify them, you have no idea how they taste. You're as much in the dark as Alice was in Wonderland when she drank from the bottle marked "Drink Me."

A tasting party is a simple way to clear up the confusion. Choose a theme—fish, fruit, desserts, mixed grill, blender drinks, sandwiches, pastas—even beans! Then orchestrate the meal so you can compare and note your preferences and dislikes, if any. The keys are small portions and plenty of water.

Like the cocktail party, a tasting party can travel from room to room, from inside to outside or simply from table to buffet to breakfront—with sampling stations at each place. For an elegant touch, buy a half dozen porcelain name cards that you can write on. Identify each dish on the name card and decorate each station with its own set of blooms and colors. If whimsy is what you're after, buy as many helium balloons as you have dishes and write the names of the foods to be tasted on the balloons.

The parties that follow illustrate the range of what you can do with a tasting party, from creating an atmosphere of casual elegance to one of unabashed childishness.

MENU

FOR 5 OR MORE

CHOCOLATE CAKE
WITH GANACHE
GLAZE

BB'S BISCOTTI

BUTTERMILK
POUND CAKE

MIRABELLE'S
ORANGE RINDS

MIXED BERRY
TART

DEBAUCHING DESSERTS

Date: December 17
Occasion: Saturnalia

In ancient Rome Saturnalia meant a day of debauchery, a day when slaves sat down with their masters, when work stopped and the people paid homage to Saturn, the god of seed sowing and the harvest. Rather than plan a party with a cornucopia and the fruits of the harvest, we've come up with a party of indulgence, of sensuous smells and sights. (On the practical side, any leftovers make perfect snacks for holiday drop-in guests, and the party can accommodate up to a dozen people.)

This is the party that deserves your best silver, white linen and lace. For that feeling of extravagance, buy cymbidium orchids to adorn the pound cake platter; nasturtiums or violets for the chocolate cake; rosebuds for the biscotti (take a cue from an East Indian tradition and create a design on a pale tablecloth from flower petals); lilies for the fruit tart; and birds of paradise for the orange rinds.

Arrange each station as if it were the only one; each table should make its own statement. Experiment. Try bronze candlesticks with patina green candles and a pale green raw silk cloth for the biscotti. White lace atop white velvet captures the essence of traditional white-on-white design, a softness that goes well with crystal candlesticks, smooth white tapers and the paleness of the cymbidium orchids. Use a burgundy and cream chintz or taffeta for the fruit tart and perhaps a splashy green, purple and orange print for the orange rinds.

Use remnants of material, just tuck the ends under. Skew the fabric, too, so it sits on the serving tops at odd, interesting angles. Because you're setting a scene rather than a table, you don't need much cloth. One station might be on a desk, another on a mantelpiece. Wherever they are, wrap a small present for each guest using fabric and gold cord, sequins or cloth ribbon. Your guests will find their gift—a custom that dates back to the first Saturnalia festivities—as they taste their way through your house.

Vary the gifts, matching each to the personality of the recipient. Consider giving a charm from the 1930s, a seashell, a delicate ribbon coiled inside a marbled box, bath oil, a compact disc or an antique pencil sharpener.

B B Bralower, a wine consultant in Roslyn, New York, whose recipes give breath to this party, is a consummate host-

© Burke/Triolo

Creating a mood may be as simple as buying fabric and trimmings. The candelabra and tableware only serve to accent the atmosphere already established by the draped material and bows.

ess. She brings to these desserts a wisdom that you can almost taste. As an example to all good cooks, B B took what are considered standard recipes and adapted them to suit her individual palate—with one notable exception. She recognized the simple goodness of chef Guy Reuge's (owner of the restaurant Mirabelle in St. James, Long Island, New York) orange rinds and has

since incorporated his recipe into her own repertoire.

As you entertain more and more, you'll develop a personal style just as B B did. Keep a record of your favorite recipes. Most likely you will take the step that makes a good cook great: You'll begin to generate your own distinctive variations on the original.

© Steven Mark Needham/Envision

CHOCOLATE CAKE

14 to 16 ounces of bittersweet chocolate	6 eggs
8 ounces (2 sticks) unsalted butter, cut up into 8 pieces	½ cup sugar
	⅓ cup all-purpose flour (optional)

Preheat oven to 425°.

Use an 8½- to 9-inch springform pan. Wrap the outside of the springform pan in aluminum to prevent water from seeping in while the pan is in a water bath. Butter the bottom of the pan and line it with wax or parchment paper. Butter the paper. Set aside.

Break the chocolate into pieces and combine it with the butter in the top of a double boiler over simmering (not boiling) water. Stir occasionally until the chocolate and butter have melted together and formed a smooth mixture.

Put the eggs into a large mixer bowl under a standing mixer and start whipping, adding the sugar gradually while you're whipping. Whip for about 8 minutes, until the mixture is about three times its original volume. The mixture should form soft peaks that are not yet dry. (If you don't have a standing mixer, warm the egg yolks over hot water before adding, beating all the while.) Fold the chocolate into the eggs, then turn the standing mixer onto low or mix by hand until no streaks remain. Sift the flour over the top of the mixture, and fold it in.

Pour the batter into the prepared pan and place the filled pan in a larger roasting pan with enough hot water so it comes halfway up the outside of the springform pan. Bake for about 7 minutes, then cover the top of the springform pan loosely with lightly buttered foil. Bake for another 15 to

20 minutes. The cake may not look done, but it will be. Remove the cake from the oven and cool in the pan for one hour. Refrigerate in the springform pan for at least two to three hours. Unmold it and carefully remove the springform. Invert the cake onto a piece of plastic wrap or parchment paper. Remove the wax paper from the bottom of the cake, then invert the cake again onto a serving platter. (You can cover and refrigerate the cake for a week at this stage.)

Sprinkle powdered sugar on top or glaze with ganache glaze.

GANACHE GLAZE

6 ounces bittersweet chocolate   2/3 cup heavy whipping cream

Break the chocolate into pieces and set aside. Heat the whipping cream over low heat and remove from the stove just as it comes to a boil. Add the chocolate to the heated cream and stir. Let the mixture sit until tepid, stir again, then pour over the cake, letting it drip artfully down the sides. To give the cake a neater appearance, put wax paper underneath the cake to catch the drips when you glaze it, then remove the paper before serving.

Let the cake sit at room temperature for 3 hours or overnight. Serve with whipped cream or decorate the top of the cake with raspberries, candied violets, and/or chocolate leaves. Or try using fresh flowers such as nasturtiums.

CHOCOLATE LEAVES

8 to 10 rose leaves or lemon leaves   1 ounce bittersweet chocolate

Pick out leaves with well-defined veining and no apparent tears or holes. Wash each one carefully. Pat dry. Line a cookie sheet with wax paper and set aside.

Melt the chocolate in a double boiler or in the microwave on 50 percent power for two to three minutes. With the back of the spoon, gather the melted chocolate and transfer it to the *back* of the leaf, where the veins are most prominent. Put the finished leaves onto the lined cookie sheet and freeze. When you are ready to decorate the cake, simply peel the leaf away from the chocolate.

You should end up with at least six good leaves.

BB'S BISCOTTI

10 ounces of unblanched almonds (preferably whole)	Pinch of salt
4 cups all-purpose flour	3 tablespoons of unsalted butter
1/2 cup firmly packed brown sugar	4 eggs
1 1/2 cups white sugar	1 cup golden raisins
1 teaspoon cinnamon	1 egg white, slightly beaten
1 teaspoon baking powder	

Preheat oven to 375°.

(This recipe works well with a standing mixer, but you can beat the ingredients in by hand without altering the results.)

Spread the almonds out on a cookie sheet and place in the preheated oven until toasted, about 15 minutes. Grind 3 ounces of the toasted almonds until fine, using a Mouli or similar grater. (If you use a food processor, add a generous pinch or two of the white sugar so the almonds don't get pasty.) Put the flour, sugar, cinnamon, baking powder and salt in the bowl and combine. Add the butter and mix well. Make a well in the center and add the eggs. Mix until it comes together.

Knead the dough for 10 to 15 minutes by hand or for 8 to 10 minutes with a dough hook on a standing mixer or for 1 to 2 minutes with the dough attachment on a food processor.

Add the remaining almonds, kneading them into the dough for about 15 seconds with a food processor or 1 minute with a dough hook in a standing mixer. Add the raisins, kneading them in by hand.

Butter and flour 2 large cookie sheets. Flour your hands and the countertop or work area. Divide the dough into 8 pieces, shaping it with your hands into long rolls 3/4 inch in diameter and 17 inches long (the length of the cookie sheet). Place the rolls on the cookie sheets with room between each one. Brush the tops with egg white.

Bake 18 to 20 minutes until lightly browned. Remove onto a board and let the rolls cool about 5 minutes. Slice each of the rolls on the diagonal, making pieces about 1/2 inch thick.

Lower the oven to 275°. Return the slices to the cookie sheets and bake an additional 35 to 40 minutes. *Biscotti* means "twice cooked."

They can be kept for a month in a well-sealed tin, or they can be frozen. Serve with blueberry ice cream or fresh fruit salad. Makes about 80 or 90 pieces.

BUTTERMILK POUND CAKE

1 cup plus 2 tablespoons unsalted butter	1 cup buttermilk
2 cups sugar	2 teaspoons vanilla
4 large eggs at room temperature	1 tablespoon grated orange rind (optional)
2 1/2 cups all-purpose flour	**For the fruit filling (optional)**
1 teaspoon baking powder	2 apples
1/2 teaspoon baking soda	2 teaspoons lemon juice
1/2 teaspoon salt	Cinnamon and sugar mixed

Preheat oven to 350°.

In a large bowl, cream 2 sticks of butter with the sugar, adding the sugar a little at a time. Beat until light. Add eggs one at a time, beating well after each.

In another bowl, sift together flour, baking powder, baking soda and salt. Add the dry ingredients to the butter mixture, a little at a time, alternating with the buttermilk. Finish by adding the last of the dry ingredients. Mix well. Stir in the vanilla and grated rind.

Fill a bundt pan or angel food pan with the batter. Rap the pan to settle the batter. Cook for 1 hour, or until a skewer comes out clean. Let cool in the pan on a rack for 20 minutes. Turn onto the rack and cool completely. This cake can be frozen or made the day before.

If adding the optional fruit filling, only fill the pan three quarters full. Slice the apples, and in a small bowl mix the fruit with the lemon juice. Layer the fruit onto the batter, then sprinkle with cinnamon-sugar. Add the remaining batter on top of the fruit. Rap the pan to settle the batter and cook for 70 minutes. Cool as above. (You can vary the fruit filling by using 2 pears, 2 peaches or 4 plums, in which case you'd need no lemon juice or cinnamon-sugar.)

MIRABELLE'S ORANGE RINDS

1 large navel orange	2 ounces extra bittersweet or bittersweet chocolate (optional)
2 cups sugar	

Cut the peel from the orange in strips from top to bottom, leaving the white pith and some orange flesh.

Cut the peel into ¼-inch-wide strips. Bring the strips to a boil in a 3-quart saucepan of salted water. Drain immediately. Bring the blanched peel, sugar and 4 cups water to a boil over high heat, stirring until the sugar is dissolved. Reduce the heat to medium high and cook 30 to 40 minutes until the candy thermometer reads 230°. (Don't let the sugar brown.) Drain the peel and cool on a rack. Serve when cooled or add chocolate.

To add chocolate, melt the chocolate over low heat, stirring constantly. Cool for 5 minutes, then dip one end of each peel into the chocolate and arrange on a lightly oiled baking sheet or wax paper. Refrigerate before serving.

Makes approximately 36 rinds.

MIXED BERRY TART

For the piecrust

1 ½ cups all-purpose flour

1 ½ sticks cold unsweetened butter

1 tablespoon sugar

Pinch of salt

Ice water (2 to 4 tablespoons, or as needed)

Combine flour, butter, sugar and salt into a food processor fitted with a steel blade. Pulse about 15 to 20 times, until dough is almost together. Begin adding 2 tablespoons of water, pulsing on and off about 10 times until the dough looks like pea-sized cornmeal. (Do not process it into a ball.)

Flour your hands. Pat the dough into a disk about 6 inches across. Refrigerate for 15 to 20 minutes before rolling out. (You can also refrigerate the dough overnight, continuing the recipe the next day.)

Flour your rolling board or work surface. Roll dough into 4-inch circles, ⅛-inch thin (or, if you're unused to rolling, ¼-inch-thin). Use a 4-inch tart top to cut out shapes. If not making the tarts immediately, put wax paper between each crust and wrap in foil. You can freeze the individual crusts for up to six months in your freezer. Makes 12 individual tart crusts.

For the berry filling

2 ½ cups fresh blueberries, raspberries and blackberries (you may also use frozen raspberries and blueberries packaged without syrup)

2 tablespoons sugar

12 individual tart crusts (see recipe above)

4 tablespoons butter

Preheat oven to 375°.

Butter a cookie sheet or jelly roll pan. Pick through the raspberries but don't wash them. Rinse the blueberries and blackberries, then pat dry.

Using either fresh or defrosted tart crusts, sprinkle the dough with approximately 1 tablespoon sugar. Starting about ¼ inch from the edge of the tart crust, make a ring of raspberries, then blackberries. Fill in the center with blueberries. Sprinkle another tablespoon of sugar on top of the berries and dot each tart with 1 teaspoon butter.

Bake the tarts until lightly browned, approximately 20 minutes. (Other fruits may be substituted: apples with apricot jam, small plums or pears.)

Melba sauce

1 cup raspberries

Framboise or lemon juice to taste

Puree the raspberries with the framboise or lemon juice. Heat over low flame before serving. Pour over the hot tarts and eat immediately.

MENU

FOR 6

FISH EN
PAPILLOTE

TUNA STARS

ORBITING FRUITS

SAUTEED STAR
FRUIT

BOW AND ARROW
COOKIES

MIDNIGHT MADNESS

Date: October 21
Occasion: Orionid meteor shower

Ideally a party for four adults and two kids, Midnight Madness can easily be a romantic gathering for two or four. The mood reflects the event: Either way, you become starstruck. Have fun with the invitations. Cut out shapes of the planets, ask the kids to color them in and enclose them in an envelope with some glittery stars (you can get them at most party stores).

The Orionid meteor shower is just one of the many showers that occur throughout the year. Check one of the farmer's almanacs for specific dates, but look for them around January 4, April 21, July 29, August 12, October 21, November 16, and December 13. Each shower originates from a specific constellation or group of stars. The best shows—the nights when the stars blaze across the sky, leaving glowing trails—happen when the moon is new and city lights are far behind you.

If the weather is warm, you might consider serving this meal outdoors, but more than likely you'll be eating inside. Set the food up as a buffet. Place little flags standing in clay to the side of each package of fish, identifying what it is. The star-shaped sandwiches are for the kids, but the menu is flexible.

The only last-minute cooking you'll be doing is sautéeing the star fruit; bring it out on a big platter and let everyone help themselves. The fruit, the candy and the cookies can be tucked into pockets for snacking outside.

Head outdoors around midnight. Gather together a plastic tarp or sheet (because the ground may be damp) and sleeping bags. Remind your guests to bundle up if you're in the colder climes. And settle down for a night of stargazing.

© Alan McClure

Because meteor showers, comets and eclipses fall on specific, calculable days, they make great party dates. Just be sure to have back-up plans in case of inclement weather.

FISH EN PAPILLOTE

4 four- to six-ounce fillets of
assorted fish: monkfish, pom-
pano, mahi-mahi and bluefish

2 lemons

4 to 6 teaspoons butter

Preheat the oven to 400°.

Cut out as many heart-shaped pieces of parchment paper as you have fillets of fish. Rinse the fish and place each fillet on the left-hand side of a parchment heart. Cut one lemon in half and rub the lemon on each piece of fish. Slice the other lemon and place one thick or two thin slices on top of each fillet. Place one teaspoon of butter on top of the lemon on each piece of fish, then close the hearts by pinching the edges into a seam. The seal should be airtight to enclose the steam.

Bake on an unbuttered baking sheet for 8 to 12 minutes. The thickness of the fish determines the baking time. Using a basic rule of thumb, cook fish that is one inch thick for 10 minutes, thinner pieces for 8 minutes, thicker pieces for 12 minutes.

Open the pockets just before eating.

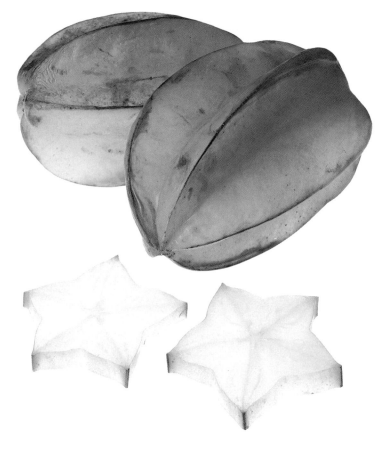

SAUTÉED STAR FRUIT

2 star fruits

1 tablespoon brown sugar

2 to 4 tablespoons butter

Wash the star fruit and slice into pieces approximately $1/2$ inch thick. Melt 2 tablespoons of butter in a large sauté pan; add the brown sugar and mix. (Depending on the size of your pan, use more or less butter.) Sauté the star fruit for 10 minutes, turning the pieces after 5 minutes. Serve warm.

TUNA STARS

One 6½ ounce can tuna fish

½ lemon

2 tablespoons mayonnaise

2 ribs celery

½ small red bell pepper

2 to 4 teaspoons fresh dill

8 pieces soft wheat bread

Drain the tuna and flake. Squeeze the lemon into the tuna and mix. Add the mayonnaise and mash slightly.

Wash the celery, pepper and dill. Pat the dill between two pieces of paper towel to dry. Chop the celery and pepper into bite-size pieces; mix into tuna. Snip the dill, using a pair of kitchen shears, into the salad and mix well. Spread onto the sandwich bread to make four sandwiches. Using star-shaped cookie cutters, cut out four sandwiches.

ORBITING FRUITS

An assortment of fruit (at least 6 pieces, more if strawberries are used)

A wire hanger

String or thin cloth ribbon

More a kid's project than a recipe, making orbiting fruits simply involves stringing the fruit up on a round wire as a mobile. Use a lady apple, a larger apple, one or two kinds of pear, an orange, a few strawberries, if they're still in the market, and whatever else will appeal to the kids. String them up gently, scoring the fruit and placing the string along the scores if necessary. Have the children cut down their fruit planets at the end of the meal.

BOW AND ARROW COOKIES

1½ cups butter

2 cups sugar

4 eggs

4 cups sifted flour

4 teaspoons baking powder

1 teaspoon vanilla

Cream the butter and sugar together, mixing well. In a small bowl, beat the eggs. Add them to the butter-sugar mixture. Sift the flour with the baking powder into the butter-sugar mixture, and stir to combine. Add the vanilla, then mix well. Cover the bowl with plastic wrap and chill in the refrigerator overnight.

Preheat the oven to 400° before you remove the cookie dough from the refrigerator. Roll the dough out and cut bow, arrow and star shapes freehand. Bake the cookies on a lightly buttered sheet until golden, about 10 minutes. Cool.

DANCING PARTIES

Anna and the King of Siam danced. Cinderella and her prince danced. Fred and Ginger danced. They danced alone in a crowd. Who says dancing parties must be huge affairs? Take advantage of the intimacy of a small group for your next dancing party.

Music is of prime importance at a dancing party. Make sure that in your master schedule you've allowed enough time to make a tape. (Tapes are easier to handle than records at a party, and they don't skip and jump if someone at the party does. You also have more freedom to mix and match than you would if you used compact discs.) Take pains to give the party a leisurely pace; dancing even at its most frenzied should be within a time warp of abandon.

If you're eating before dancing, plan a light meal followed by a group diversion before everyone takes to their feet. You might also want to change dessert and a postprandial drink into an after-dancing event, a sweet close to the evening. If you're dancing before eating, set up a small bar with small munchies—popcorn, mixed nuts or other classics.

Space, too, takes on greater importance than it normally would. You want things cozy enough for dinner but spacious enough for people to let loose a little. Batten down the hatches. Roll up the rugs. And free yourself from having to think about all the little odds and ends that could break.

MENU

FOR 6

SCREAMING
WINGS

STUFFED SGT.
PEPPERS

PEACE PIE

SIXTIES SALAD

STRAWBERRY
COEUR A LA
CREME

SIXTIES BASH

Date: February 7, 1964
Occasion: The Beatles arrived in the United States

Less than two weeks after the Beatles released "Love Me Do," their first hit record climbed to number one. Shortly thereafter, Ed Sullivan, inadvertently delayed by a horde of screaming Beatles fans at the London airport, signed the group—unknown in the States—to appear on his show. By the time the Beatles walked out of the BOAC plane at Kennedy Airport on February 7, 1964, they were already stars. Their music had preceded them.

And their music is integral to a nostalgic bash. Get your hands on at least four or five of their albums—some now available on compact disc—to play before and after dinner. Design the invitations around the song "A Ticket to Ride" and pick each guest up to take them to the party. Set the table with homemade miniature scenarios for each guest to take home: an octopus in a fluorescent garden; a yellow submarine in a small fishbowl; a portrait of "Lucy" framed in a black box studded with rhinestone "diamonds", a weeping guitar; a barber selling photographs; a field of strawberries. If you don't feel the creative urge, skip the scenarios and focus on the music. It will carry the party.

Ask your friends to bring any Beatles memorabilia they might have: books, posters, wigs, dolls, shirts. Buy a small roll of clear vinyl and cut pieces to a size larger and longer than that of an album cover. Sew together two or three sides with embroidery thread or yarn, and slip empty album covers inside to use as placemats.

Call a local radio station and request a greeting and a song to start off the dancing (you may have to call in advance and explain what you're doing). You won't need much space for six people, but be sure you've cleared anything that's breakable from the dance area.

If you're lacking memorabilia, combine the Beatles bash with another party idea based on things from the past: a swap party. Explain to friends that each person should bring at least one item—usually clothing—in good condition for swapping. You can then auction off each piece one at a time, using other items as the currency. To vary the idea, guests can bring antiques such as pewter ice-cream molds, baby quilts or spongeware; if you opt for this, set an approximate value for the items to be brought.

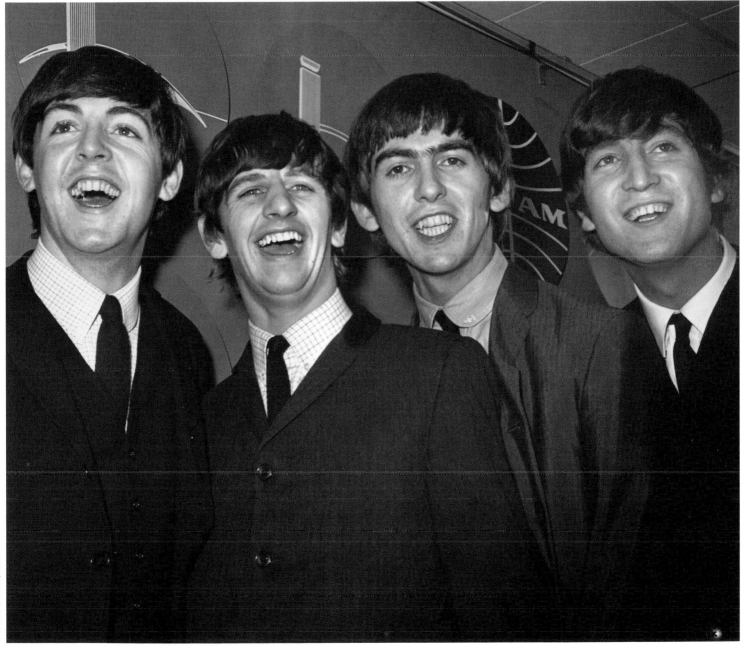

SCREAMING WINGS

12 chicken wings

1 cup melted butter

Tabasco™ sauce to taste

Salt to taste

Pepper to taste

Vegetable oil for frying

Clean chicken wings and cut into thirds, discarding the tips. Mix the butter, Tabasco™ sauce, salt and pepper in a large bowl. Toss the wings in the seasoning until well covered. Deep fry at 350° for 12 minutes.

(For a crispy version, combine ⅓ cup dry sherry, ⅓ cup soy sauce and ⅔ cup cornstarch; toss the wings in; and deep fry as above.)

© Gordon E. Smith

STUFFED SGT. PEPPERS

2 peppers (Anaheim peppers are best)

1 pound of sweet or hot sausage, cooked

Tomato juice

Salt to taste

Pepper to taste

Preheat the oven to 350°.

Clean the peppers and core them by slicing off the top and pulling out the core. Remove any seeds. Pack the sausage into the interior of the peppers, leaving no air gaps. Stand the peppers up in a casserole dish. Season the tomato juice with pepper and salt, and pour just enough into the casserole dish to cover the bottom. Cook, covered, for 25 minutes.

Remove the peppers from the oven and transfer them onto a platter. Cool. When thoroughly cooled, slice the peppers into stuffed rings and serve on homemade rye crackers.

Rye crackers

6 tablespoons oil

2 teaspoons salt

2 cups rye flour

¼ cup sesame seeds

¼ cup brown sugar

Mix all the ingredients together with ½ cup water, kneading the dough slightly. Roll the dough out very thin. Cut into squares slightly larger than the width of the peppers. Touch fork to the dough, making several holes, and bake for 12 to 15 minutes at 350°.

PEACE PIE

2 to 3 pounds lamb with bones

Salt to taste

Pepper to taste

Butter or oil to sear

1 carrot

2 medium onions

2 ribs celery

Roux (see recipe below)

4 potatoes

6 spears asparagus

Fresh rosemary sprigs

Frozen pie shell

For the roux:

1 tablespoon butter

1 tablespoon flour

1 cup lamb stock

Dice the raw lamb meat into ¼-inch cubes; save the lamb bones and scraps for stock. Sprinkle the diced lamb with salt and pepper. Sear the lamb in butter or oil to brown but not cook fully. Cool immediately and reserve.

Put the lamb bones and scraps into a stock pot and cover with cold water. Chop the carrot, 1 onion and celery and add to the stock. Bring to a boil, skim off the scum that comes to the top and simmer for 5 hours, skimming as needed.

Melt the butter over medium heat in a small sauté pan. Whisk in the flour. When blended, gradually whisk in the hot lamb stock and simmer the mixture for 20 minutes, stirring frequently. Season with salt and pepper.

Preheat the oven to 325°.

Dice the raw potatoes and second onion. Cut the asparagus on the diagonal into 2-inch pieces. Mix the vegetables with the seared lamb and fresh rosemary. Put the lamb and vegetable mixture into the pie shell. Cover with the roux-thickened stock and bake for 25 minutes uncovered.

SIXTIES SALAD

1 cup flour

2 tablespoons fresh cracked black pepper

1 egg

1 egg yolk

2 tablespoons melted butter

$\frac{1}{3}$ cup mung bean sprouts

$\frac{1}{3}$ cup alfalfa sprouts

4 to 5 scallions

Sesame seeds to garnish

Mix together the flour and cracked pepper and turn out onto a flat work surface. Make a ring of the pepper-flour and a well in the center for the egg, egg yolk and melted butter. Work the eggs and butter into the flour until combined. Knead for 4 minutes. Rest the dough, covered, for 1 hour or more. Using a hand-crank pasta machine, cut into wide noodles on a no. 2 setting. Cook noodles in boiling water until al dente, about 3 or 4 minutes (longer, if not using homemade pasta). Drain and cool.

Toss the pasta with the sprouts, scallions and sesame seeds. Add the tahini dressing and toss again.

Tahini dressing

$\frac{1}{2}$ cup tahini

$\frac{1}{4}$ cup olive oil

$\frac{1}{3}$ cup lemon juice

$\frac{1}{4}$ teaspoon salt

In a blender, combine all of the ingredients. Add a few teaspoons of water, blending as you add until you get a smooth, medium thick consistency. Let dressing sit for 20 minutes or more before serving.

Makes about 1$\frac{1}{4}$ cups.

STRAWBERRY COEUR A LA CREME

1 pound cottage cheese

1 pound cream cheese

Pinch of salt

¼ cup sugar

1 tablespoon confectioners' sugar

2 cups heavy cream

2 cups crushed strawberries

Whole strawberries for garnish

Rinse enough cheesecloth to line 6 individual or 2 regular-size heart-shaped coeur a la creme molds (see Sources, pages 138 to 139). Squeeze out any excess water without destroying the matrix of the cheesecloth and line each mold.

Using an electric mixer, combine the cottage cheese, cream cheese, and salt thoroughly. Add in the sugar and beat well; gradually add the heavy cream and beat until smooth.

Spoon the mixture into the lined molds. Refrigerate overnight on a plate that's deep enough to catch the draining liquid.

Just before serving, combine the crushed strawberries with the confectioners' sugar. When ready to serve, unmold the hearts onto chilled plates and serve with sweetened, crushed strawberries. Garnish with whole strawberries.

MENU

FOR 8

BRIE WITH RED
PEPPERS AND
OLIVES

ANGEL BISCUITS

SHRIMP AND
CHICKEN
SKEWERS

GUACAMOLE

CELERY ROOT
AND RED
CABBAGE RAVE

BAKED SWEET
AND IDAHO
POTATO CHIPS

CHOCOLATE-DIPPED
PECAN
SHORTBREAD

MOVING PARTY

Date: You supply the date
Occasion: When someone moves

What better time to have a dancing party than when all the rooms are cleared and nothing's in the way! Ideally, someone other than the person moving should actually plan the party; the ordeal of moving is enough to think about. Yet, with helping hands setting up the food and cleaning up, this becomes a hassle-free party. Send invitations on torn pieces of paper bag, written in magic marker.

Portability is the leitmotif of this party. For the dancing, bring tapes and a boombox. For the food, pack a large flat-bottomed basket. On the bottommost layer, place a small, sturdy box of crackers, tinned smoked oysters or pâté, Teuscher chocolates, a tangerine and a small pear or two, a corkscrew, a half bottle of champagne, and a small cut-crystal bud vase. That layer stays put as a surprise present for the person who's moving. On top of that pack paper plates, real forks and cups. On top of the gift layer, pack the day's party food.

Hollow out a cabbage large enough to hold the guacamole dip in a small glass container (an empty 8-ounce jar works well).

That way you can seal the guacamole with the jar's cover but still keep it in a ready-to serve form. Wrap the finished skewers in plastic wrap and aluminum foil. To set up for the party, stick each skewer (preferably of disposable wood) end into the cabbage. Save the Brie box; the top half of the box can hold the cheese; the bottom half can hold the celery root and red cabbage rave. Mold a piece of aluminum foil to the other half of the wheel, forming a dam of sorts to separate the cheese from the cabbage salad, which you can transport in a plastic bag. Carry the angel biscuits in a paper bag with handles, which you can later use for trash. Line the bottom of the paper bag with a folded plastic bag that will double as an

inner trash bag. The paper bag can also hold the potato chips, carried in a smaller paper bag, and aluminum foil-wrapped shortbread. Tuck a sheet into the top of the basket; it can double as a tablecloth. The only other party items to bring are beer and soft drinks, which can be packed up and dropped off at a bottle-return center.

If coffee drinkers can't do without a fix, Carrie Levin and Ann Nickinson (owners of the Good Enough to Eat restaurants in New York City, and High Falls, New York) suggest the host make very strong coffee and freeze it in an ice-cube tray. Take the cubes to the party and when your guests crave coffee, serve iced coffee with milk.

To set the scene, invest in a few colorful streamers and balloons. Both pack small and can be cleaned up quickly and easily.

Shades of Lawrence Welk! But it's great fun to bring along a few bottles of soap bubbles to start off the dancing. Take turns making bubbles while you continue to dance until the music takes over. Big band music fills up an empty space; New Orleans zydeco is great too. My particular favorites are Jonah Jones's *Jumpin with Jonah*, and the Neville Brothers' *Nevillization*. Pick a menu of ethnic songs as a change from American rock or pop: Theodore Bikel, the Gypsy Kings, Gato Barbieri and Hugh Masekela.

A Moving Party is perfect for when the packing is done and the truck is ready to leave. Friends of the person who is moving should take care of the planning, but overall, this is a hassle-free party that doesn't require too much work.

BRIE WITH RED PEPPERS AND OLIVES

½ wheel Brie

2 large peppers

Olive oil

Fresh or dried *herbes de Provence* to taste

Assorted olives

Lay each pepper on a burner of the stove, and over high flame or heat roast them, turning them with a long-handled fork or tongs until the skin blackens and the flesh becomes tender but not mushy.

Remove the peppers from the heat and transfer them to a brown paper bag. Allow them to cool for about 15 minutes in the bag. Take the peppers from the bag; the skin should peel off easily. Remove the peel, and discard the core and the seeds. Slice the peppers into ½-inch-thick pieces and put them in a mixing bowl. Add just enough olive oil to cover, then sprinkle with herbs.

Arrange the pepper strips and the olives on top of the Brie. To serve, cut the Brie in its wheel box as you would cut a pie in its baking dish.

ANGEL BISCUITS

1 tablespoon dried yeast

1 tablespoon plus a pinch of sugar

⅛ cup tepid water

2½ cups all-purpose flour

1 tablespoon baking powder

⅛ teaspoon baking soda

¼ teaspoon salt

½ cup vegetable shortening

⅔ cup buttermilk, at room temperature

Flour for the biscuit cutter

Melted butter to brush tops

In a small bowl, dissolve the yeast with a pinch of the sugar in the tepid water. Preheat the oven to 350°, and lightly grease a baking sheet.

Combine the flour, baking powder, baking soda, tablespoon of sugar and salt in a large mixing bowl. To prevent overhandling of the dough, use 2 knives to cut in the shortening until it resembles coarse meal. Add the yeast mixture. Then add the buttermilk and bring the dough together with your hands in a light kneading movement, making sure no dry ingredients have settled to the bottom of the bowl.

Turn the dough out onto a very lightly floured surface, and pat it out 1 to 1¼ inches thick. Dip a 2-inch biscuit cutter into the flour before each cut. Cut, then place immediately on the baking sheet. With the side of the biscuit cutter, push the dough together as you work, keeping it all in one piece. Handle the dough as little as possible.

If you like soft biscuits, crowd them close together on the baking sheets so the sides don't become crusty; if you like crusty biscuits, bake them far apart. Bake for 18 to 20 minutes or until their tops turn golden. Remove them from the oven and brush their tops with melted butter.

Yields 12 biscuits.

© Steve \ Mark Needham/Envision

SHRIMP AND CHICKEN SKEWERS

Fresh or dried *herbes de Provence*

2 cups dry white wine

2 boned chicken breasts

18 large shrimp

Combine 1 cup of the wine and half of the herbs in a non-reactive frying pan. Add enough water so that once the chicken breasts are added, they will be covered. Bring the poaching liquid to a low boil. Place the chicken breasts carefully into the poaching liquid, and reduce the heat to a low simmer. Poach for 11 minutes. Drain the chicken and cut into large chunks.

Repeat the poaching process using the shrimp instead of the chicken. (You'll need less water and the wine flavor will become more pronounced.)

Arrange each shrimp and chicken piece on a skewer and, once cool, refrigerate until 15 minutes or so before serving.

GUACAMOLE

1 plum tomato

1 clove garlic, chopped

½ teaspoon chopped fresh cilantro

¼ teaspoon kosher salt

½ teaspoon black pepper

Pinch of cayenne pepper

1 drop hot pepper sauce

1 teaspoon freshly squeezed lime juice

1 ripe avocado

To peel the tomato, core it from the top, then cut a cross in the bottom. Using a skimmer or slotted spoon, dip it into boiling water for 8 seconds and remove. Cool. The peel should slip off easily. Cut the tomato in half, then gently squeeze each half to remove the seeds. Chop fine.

If using a mini food processor, place the garlic, cilantro, salt, pepper, cayenne, hot pepper sauce and lime juice in a bowl and process until combined. Peel and pit the avocado and tomato, add them to the other ingredients and process until just combined.

If making the guacamole by hand, grind the garlic with salt and pepper using a mortar and pestle. Peel, pit and mash the avocado in a separate bowl, gradually mashing in the remaining ingredients. Place the avocado pit in the guacamole to prevent it from browning.

Let sit at room temperature for ½ hour before serving.

Makes approximately 1 cup.

CELERY ROOT AND RED CABBAGE RAVE

¾ pound celery root, peeled

1 medium head red cabbage

1 egg yolk

¾ teaspoon kosher salt

½ teaspoon white pepper

⅛ cup Dijon mustard

1 tablespoon fresh lemon juice

½ tablespoon white wine

1 cup olive oil

½ tablespoon caraway seeds

Place the celery root in a mixing bowl. Wash the cabbage. Shred three quarters of the cabbage, saving about 6 outer leaves for presentation, and add to the celery root.

To prepare the dressing, place the yolk in the blender bowl of a food processor, add salt, pepper, mustard, lemon juice and whisk by hand, scraping down the sides of the bowl, until well blended. Then, with the food processor on, drizzle in the white wine. Gradually drizzle in the olive oil, a drop at a time, completely incorporating the drop before adding more. The mayonnaise should be emulsified before two thirds of the olive oil is used.

Mix the dressing in with the celery root and cabbage. Sprinkle on the caraway seeds, then toss. Let the salad sit, refrigerated, for at least 2 hours before serving.

© Martin Rogers/FPG International

BAKED SWEET AND IDAHO POTATO CHIPS

¼ cup pure olive oil (not extra-virgin)

1 teaspoon kosher salt

¾ teaspoon dried thyme, crushed

¼ teaspoon ground ginger

1 pound Idaho potatoes

1 pound sweet potatoes

Preheat oven to 375°.

Line baking sheets with parchment paper. Combine the oil, salt, thyme and ginger in a large bowl; set aside.

Wash and dry the potatoes. Without peeling the vitamin-packed skins, but after removing any blemishes, slice the Idaho potatoes into ¼-inch-thick circles. Place them in the oil mixture and stir to coat them well. Wash and slice the sweet potatoes into ½-inch-thick circles, and coat them with the oil mixture, too.

Place the potatoes on the prepared baking sheets in a single layer and roast 20 to 25 minutes, until lightly browned.

CHOCOLATE-DIPPED PECAN SHORTBREAD

1 1/2 cups all-purpose flour

1/2 cup sugar

1/2 cup ground pecans
(1/4 pound)

10 1/2 tablespoons sweet butter,
softened

3 ounces semisweet chocolate

1/2 cup shredded coconut,
toasted

Preheat the oven to 350°.

Combine the flour, sugar and pecans in a mixing bowl. Cut in the butter until the mixture stays together when pressed. (Shortbread should be worked lightly so it will taste the way the name suggests: short, or buttery.) Press the dough into a 9-inch round pan; score lightly with a knife into 8 equal wedges (do not cut all the way through), then prick the dough with a fork in even rows on top of each wedge.

Bake 30 minutes, or until the top is light brown. Cool slightly, then separate the wedges completely with a knife. Remove the wedges by inverting them onto the bottom of another pan; then place on a wire rack to cool completely. Handle the wedges gently so they don't break.

Meanwhile, melt the chocolate in a double boiler or a microwave. When the shortbread is thoroughly cool, dip each pointed end into the chocolate. Place the wedges on a sheet of parchment paper or on a rack set over aluminum foil. Sprinkle coconut over the wedges, if you want, and let the chocolate harden.

Makes 8 one-inch wedges.

© Susanna Pashko/Envision

IMPROMPTU PARTIES

The most basic factor in hosting an impromptu party is keeping your cool. If you can do that, you can put together these two smashing parties with only one day's notice or less.

Let's take the parties one at a time. With puff pastry in the freezer and different kinds of chocolate, vanilla, sugar, flour and condensed milk in the cupboard, all you need to do is stop at a liquor store and a grocery for dairy goods, eggs, fruit and macadamia nuts. If you have only the day of the party to prepare, make the forgotten cookies first, then the puff pastry rolls, which need the higher heat. Follow with the chocolate mint squares and the on-top-of-the-stove recipes: the chocolate-dipped strawberries, the Grand Marnier strips and Irish Cream; you can add to the menu if you have an extra day or more. Alternatively, with only a few hours, you can whip together a mini-tea with the puff pastry rolls, the strawberries, the Grand Marnier strips and the Irish Cream.

MENU

FOR 7 TO 8

MIMOSAS

FRESH FRUIT
BOWL

STRAWBERRY
CREAM

OVEN-BAKED
SHRIMP AND
ARTICHOKE
HEART FRITTATA

CHEESY PECAN
BREAD

APPLE-NUT
MUFFINS
ORANGE BUTTER

RAINY DAY BRUNCH

Date: July 15
Occasion: St. Swithin's Day

St. Swithin's Day if thou dost rain,
For forty days it will remain.
St. Swithin's Day if thou be fair,
For forty days 'twill rain na mair.
—Old English rhyme

When St. Swithin—known as the Bishop of Winchester in his day—died in the middle of the ninth century, he requested that he be buried outside his church so that he might be able to feel the cool rains. Centuries later, the Bishop was canonized and the church authorities tried to move his remains inside, as befitted a saint. The legend goes on to say that a terrible thunderstorm brought on by the saint's displeasure halted the proceedings. The rains continued for forty days, and the Bishop of Swithin stayed put. So now, if it rains on St. Swithin's Day, as the rhyme says, it will rain for 40 days. If it's clear on the saint's day, no rain will fall for those 40 days.

In memory of St. Swithin, we celebrate the rainy days. Whether you actually throw the party on St. Swithin's Day is not important. The idea is to make festive what might otherwise be a dreary rainy day. The menu is simple enough that one day's notice for guests is enough.

Eight people may call for a buffet setting. Open a laquered, Chinese umbrella, set it on its side, and tuck a basket of muffins and a bread board with the pecan bread underneath. Use a length of yellow slicker material as a runner and if you can find a clean, child's yellow or red rubber boot, use it as a wine cooler. Slip a slender vase into the boot's mate and set it at the other end of the buffet area. To add a touch of whimsy, place a wide bowl on the table with a swimming yellow duck.

Bed-and-breakfast owner Joanne Claus (of the romantic Haydon House in Healdsburg, California), who contributed the recipes, tends a brilliant garden with climbing roses, hydrangeas, and a tapestry of perennials. She also collects old lithographs. Both attest to her fine eye for entertaining. A rainy day party may be just the excuse to buy a nineteenth-century print of a day of "weather." Prop it up, framed, behind the food and adorn it with different levels of bouquets.

For music, collect as many songs about the rain as you can find on tape, but don't overwhelm the party with them.

Small parties that fit into a gazebo, greenhouse or other covered garden space can turn a rainy day into a splash. Invite folks over to enjoy being outside, but under cover, on a wet afternoon.

MIMOSAS

1 bottle (750 ml) champagne, chilled

4 cups fresh squeezed orange juice, chilled

Whole or sliced strawberries for garnish

Fresh mint for garnish

Ice cubes (optional)

Combine champagne and orange juice in chilled pitcher. Add ice cubes, if desired. Garnish with whole or sliced strawberries and mint.

© FPG International

FRESH FRUIT BOWL

8 to 12 cups fresh fruit
(peaches, nectarines, blueberries, raspberries, ripe
melon)

Juice of one lemon

Allow 1 to 1½ cups of fruit per person. Wash the fruit. Cut the melon into chunks or scoop out into balls. Slice the peaches and nectarines, place in a separate bowl and coat with lemon juice. Mix the fruit together. Spoon a generous amount of strawberry cream (see recipe below) over each serving just before bringing to the table or put the fruit and strawberry cream out together buffet style.

STRAWBERRY CREAM

1 pint whipping cream

½ cup sugar

1 teaspoon vanilla

1 small (6 oz) container of
strawberry-flavored, low-gelatin
yogurt (such as Yoplait brand)

Fresh mint sprigs

Whip the cream with the sugar and vanilla until thickened. Just prior to serving, fold in the yogurt. Keep chilled. Garnish with fresh mint.

OVEN-BAKED SHRIMP AND ARTICHOKE HEART FRITTATA

1 cup small shrimp, cooked

1½ cups Swiss cheese, grated

½ cup scallions, thinly sliced

2 cloves garlic, minced

1 cup artichoke hearts, cooked and coarsely chopped

1 teaspoon fresh or dried dill

8 eggs

¾ cup milk

½ teaspoon salt

¼ teaspoon pepper

¼ teaspoon nutmeg

In a medium bowl, mix together shrimp, grated cheese, scallions, garlic, artichoke hearts and dill. Distribute evenly in a 10-inch quiche dish.

Lightly beat the eggs with milk. Stir in salt, pepper and nutmeg. Pour over the shrimp mixture and bake at 350° for about 45 minutes, or until a knife inserted in the center comes out clean. Let stand for 10 minutes before cutting.

© Burke/Triolo

APPLE-NUT MUFFINS

1 cup all-purpose flour	1 teaspoon cinnamon
1/2 teaspoon salt	1/2 teaspoon nutmeg
1 teaspoon baking soda	1 cup walnuts, coarsely chopped
2 cups Granny Smith or Golden Delicious apples, peeled and diced	1/2 cup raisins, softened
1 egg	1 teaspoon vanilla
1/4 cup vegetable oil	1/2 cup shredded coconut (optional)
3/4 cup sugar	Confectioners' sugar

Preheat the oven to 350°.

Combine the flour, salt and baking soda. In a large bowl, mix the remaining ingredients, except for the confectioners' sugar, together until well combined. Add the flour mixture to the apple mixture and blend until moistened. Spoon batter into muffin cups (three-quarters full) and bake 30 to 35 minutes.

Cool in the pan for several minutes, then dust the warm muffins with confectioners' sugar. Serve with orange butter.

Makes 12 muffins.

ORANGE BUTTER

3 ounces butter

8 ounces cream cheese

2/3 cup confectioners' sugar

2 tablespoons grated orange rind

Approximately 1 tablespoon orange juice

Soften the butter and cream cheese to room temperature; beat until smooth. Add the confectioners' sugar, orange rind and orange juice to the butter and cream cheese combination. Mix together until smooth or of desired consistency (use the orange juice to vary the consistency).

Refrigerate and use any leftover butter during the next week.

CHEESY PECAN BREAD

3 cups all-purpose flour

2/3 cup sugar

1/2 cup Parmesan cheese, grated

4 teaspoons baking powder

1/2 teaspoon salt

1 egg, beaten

1 3/4 cups milk

1/3 cup cooking oil

1 cup pecans, chopped

Preheat the oven to 350°.

Mix together the flour, sugar, cheese, baking powder and salt in a large mixing bowl. In a separate bowl, mix together egg, milk and oil. Add the egg mixture to the dry ingredients, mixing only until combined. Add 3/4 cup of the pecans. Turn into a greased 9-x-5-x-3-inch loaf pan. Sprinkle the remaining pecans over the mixture.

Bake for about 1 hour at 350°, or until a toothpick inserted into the center comes out clean. Cool in the pan for approximately 10 minutes, then remove to a wire rack and allow it to cool completely. (Keeping it overnight intensifies the flavor.)

The loaf can be frozen up to 4 months. To unfreeze, loosen the wrap slightly and thaw at room temperature.

MENU

FOR 4

PUFF PASTRY
HEARTS

CHOCOLATE
GRAND MARNIER
STRIPS

CHOCOLATE
DIPPED
STRAWBERRIES

FORGOTTEN
COOKIES

PUFF PASTRY
ROLLS

IRISH CREAM

CHOCOLATE MINT
SQUARES

SELECTED TEAS

BEETHOVEN TEA

**Date: December 16, 1770 and 1773
Occasions: Beethoven's birthday and
the Boston Tea Party**

Disguised as Indians, a group of angry colonists boarded three ships in Boston Harbor on the night of December 16, 1773 and threw the cargo of tea into the water. A tea tax that hadn't been rescinded inspired their act; a modern-day tea party should inspire yours.

Afternoon tea has once again crept into the mainstream, proving itself as an elegant afternoon distraction. The tradition began, supposedly, with the Duchess of Bedford in the late 1700s. Her tea parties assembled at around 4 p.m. and included such delicacies as cucumber sandwiches, fruit tarts, muffins and crumpets.

Miya Patrick (owner of The Charles Hinckley House, a warm, welcoming, and refined bed and breakfast on Cape Cod) chose a sweet tea to present. To vary the menu, simply add sophisticated sandwiches made from crustless soft white bread, paper-thin cucumber slices and softened butter; or smoked fish dainties of bite-size black bread, herb mayonnaise and smoked salmon or sable.

Warm a porcelain teapot with hot tap water before adding the boiling water; rinse out; then drop in one teaspoon of loose tea per person, plus one extra. Pour the boiling water over the loose tea and let it steep, with the lid on, for four to five minutes. Tea lovers stir the tea once before straining the brew into cups. Have milk, lemon slices, honey and sugar out for those who want to add to their tea.

Go for simplicity in the decor.

Because Beethoven's birthday falls so close to the Boston Tea Party, honor the composer by playing the Pastoral, his violin concerto, some of his lesser-known sonatas and, of course, your own favorites.

Sonate № 4.

Use sheet music to set the scene for a musical part, or bring in a musician. Local colleges or children's teachers are usually an inexpensive alternative to professional services.

PUFF PASTRY HEARTS

1 cup whipping cream, plus extra for glazing (optional)

1/8 pound white chocolate, chopped

1/4 pound store-bought puff pastry

1 egg yolk, beaten, for glazing (optional)

1 kiwi

1/2 pint fresh raspberries

In a saucepan over low heat, bring the whipping cream to a light boil (be careful not to overheat). Remove from the heat immediately and add the white chocolate, stirring occasionally until melted and smooth. Let the mixture cool, then refrigerate overnight.

The next day, preheat the oven to 400°.

Roll out the puff pastry to 1/8 to 1/4 inch thick. Using a heart-shaped pastry cutter, cut out 4 heart shapes. Place the puff-pastry shapes on a cookie sheet and brush with either beaten egg yolks or whipping cream.

Bake for 20 minutes. Let cool completely. Whip the chocolate mixture to whipped cream consistency (taking care not to overmix). Slice the kiwi and place in the bottom of the heart. Spoon the chocolate mixture on top of the kiwi, then place raspberries around the top of the heart.

CHOCOLATE GRAND MARNIER STRIPS

1/8 cup whipping cream

2 1/2 ounces dark chocolate, chopped

1 tablespoon Grand Marnier

Confectioners' sugar for dusting

Line the bottom of a baking sheet with parchment paper. Heat the cream in a saucepan over low heat and bring just to a light boil (be careful not to overheat). Remove from the heat immediately and add the chocolate. Mix occasionally. When the chocolate is melted, add the Grand Marnier. Refrigerate until the mixture is firm enough to hold soft peaks.

Using a fluted tip in a pastry bag, pipe strips onto the parchment paper. Place the baking sheet with the strips on it in the freezer. Remove it from the freezer just before serving. Cut the long strips into smaller strips 1 1/2 to 2 inches long. Dust with confectioners' sugar.

© Stock Imagery

CHOCOLATE-DIPPED STRAWBERRIES

4 ounces white chocolate, chopped

20 large strawberries

6-inch Styrofoam cone with blunt top

Melt white chocolate in a double boiler. While simmering, stir until smooth.

Insert a toothpick into the green hull of a strawberry and dip the opposite end into the white chocolate. Place on a wire rack to set. Starting at the bottom of the cone and working up, stick the toothpick-skewered strawberries into the styrofoam. Place the strawberry-adorned cone on a tray with green leaves [Williams Sonoma (see Sources, pages 138 to 139) sells display leaves year round]. Chill until ready to serve.

FORGOTTEN COOKIES

1 egg white

A pinch of salt

¹/₈ cup sugar

¹/₄ teaspoon vanilla

3 ounces chocolate chips
(optional)

Preheat the oven to 375°.

Beat egg whites and salt until very stiff. Gradually add the sugar and vanilla, and again beat until stiff. Fold in the chocolate chips.

Grease a cookie sheet and drop the mixture onto the sheet by the teaspoonful. Turn the oven *off* and place the cookie sheet in the oven overnight or, if you're making the cookies early in the day, put them in the oven in the morning and remove them by dinnertime.

Note: if you make these on a rainy day, the moisture in the air will make it difficult for them to set.

PUFF PASTRY ROLLS

¹/₄ pound store-bought puff
pastry

¹/₄ cup dark chocolate,
chopped

¹/₄ cup macadamia nuts,
chopped into large pieces

Preheat the oven to 400°.

Roll out the pastry to ¹/₈- to ¹/₄-inch thick. Cut into 4- by 6-inch pieces. Place the chocolate and chopped nuts onto the pastry evenly, and roll up. Place on a cookie sheet and bake for 20 minutes.

IRISH CREAM

½ can sweetened condensed milk

½ pint half and half

½ quart premium brand chocolate ice cream

½ teaspoon vanilla

8 ounces whiskey

2 tablespoons chocolate syrup

Blend all of the ingredients together and refrigerate for at least 15 minutes.

© Burke/Triolo

CHOCOLATE MINT SQUARE CAKE

½ cup butter, softened

1 cup sugar

4 eggs, beaten

1 teaspoon vanilla

1 cup flour

½ teaspoon salt

16 ounces chocolate syrup

Preheat the oven to 350°.

Cream softened butter and sugar until mixture is light and fluffy. Add beaten eggs and vanilla, and continue to beat. Slowly add in the flour and salt. Then add the chocolate syrup and mix well. Scrape the mixture onto a greased and floured cookie sheet. Bake for 30 to 40 minutes. Add the mint topping and chocolate topping.

Mint topping

¾ cups butter, softened

3 cups confectioners' sugar

3 tablespoons creme de menthe (or mint extract and water)

Cream the butter and the sugar together. Then add the mint flavoring and mix well. Spread the mint topping over the cooled cake with a spatula and refrigerate for 1 hour.

Chocolate topping

8 ounces extra bittersweet dark chocolate

8 ounces butter

In a double boiler, melt the chocolate and the butter together. Spread evenly over the mint-topped cake and refrigerate for ½ hour. Cut into squares.

PARTY GAMES

A few years ago in a wonderfully dusty old bookshop, I found a small volume entitled *Bright Ideas for Entertaining*, written in 1905 by Mrs. Herbert B. Linscott. A time capsule, the book recommends "two hundred forms of amusement or entertainment for social gatherings of all kinds…." Its grand schemes revolved around guessing games, color themes and variations on encouraging men and women or couples to mix and mingle, most of them terribly outdated. There is, however, a certain charm captured within its pages. Hostesses wore crepe paper gowns coordinated with the decor, gave out souvenirs or prizes and insisted everyone join in the fun. Forget the poverty sociable, spelling bee, or a game named "Why We Never Married," but try infusing a little old-fashioned gamesmanship at your next party. Small parties, especially, lend themselves to parlour games.

Today's guests, jaded by high technology and sometimes complacent sophistication, need to be jolted by the unfamiliar, which in this case is a return to simplicity. The following ideas range from taking a child's activity out of context to a classic among word games.

Child's Play

Perfect for a picnic or a casual meal in a family room or kitchen, this party idea may not go over well until your guests actually hunker down and get their hands dirty. In fact, if you think you can get away with it, tell your friends only that they should wear old clothes; but don't tell them what's in store. A finger-painted invitation provides a hint.

Buy ready-made finger paints or mix your own. Provide oversized shirts or full-body aprons (from a rummage sale) just in case guests haven't followed your suggestion. Spread out a length of plastic sheeting to cover the play area, and pieces of hard cardboard if you're outside, then dig in. Whether you use homemade paints or not, consider buying a roll of plain white, glossy shelf paper and having all your guests work on one giant painting. Or, before your guests arrive, glue or staple finger-painting paper to a piece of large cardboard or wood; after everyone adds something to the painting and it's dry, store it for a party reunion in which the painting is the party backdrop (this is especially fun if you create a theme for the second party based on the finished painting—underwater, in a cave, in outer space, wherever). Especially creative adults can fashion jewelry out of the finger-painted pieces, by gluing painted shapes to a stronger surface and either shellacking them or covering them with an acrylic fixer or clear nail polish.

To indulge in the children's theme even more, put out modeling clay (on waxed paper taped down to a table or, if outside, a board), crayons, pastels, construction paper, and glue. Guests who know what's up should each bring some scraps that can be used in collages: yarn, glitter, fabric, old magazines.

Another variation focuses not on finger painting but on decorating a sheet. Depending on whether you want the sheet for a backdrop or for its intended use, set out a rainbow of fabric markers or a whole array of collage items.

Create personalized pillowcases for a new couple at their wedding shower or informal reception. In a corner or back room, so as not to distract from the main activities, arrange a table with fabric markers and white, all-cotton pillowcases. Two, even three, people can draw together, and upwards of ten can contribute to the same case. Encourage imaginations to run free by starting with a bold doodle scrawled across the entire length or begin by inking in a dainty border.

HOMEMADE
FINGER PAINTS

1 ½ cups laundry starch	1 ½ cups soap flakes
Cold water	½ cup talcum (optional)
1 quart boiling water	Assorted tempera colors

Mix the laundry starch together with the cold water until the consistency is that of a thick paste. Pour in the hot water, stirring constantly until the solution is clear and looks somewhat glossy. Let the mixture cool, then add the soap flakes and, if desired, the talcum. Keep cool until ready to use. Place the thick mixture into cupcake tins, adding the colors now.

Charades

A classic if ever there was one, charades involves pantomiming a phrase or title for another team to guess. The game usually begins with players with limited enthusiasm, who end up a gaggle of gigglers.

First, divide the group into two equal teams (it's best to play with at least eight people) and seat people in two half circles so that everyone can see the "actor" in the center. Instruct one team to come up with six titles, easily recognizable quotations, or well-known advertising slogans, giving them approximately five minutes to confer and write the titles down on separate slips of paper. Fold the papers and toss in a hat before presenting the opposing team with the hat. To play, one person from the first team (it doesn't matter who goes first) chooses a slip of paper from the hat, then acts out that title (written by the opposing team) for his own team.

Before the play begins, familiarize everyone with the rules. There are probably as many variations to charades as there are recipes for apple pie.

1) The actor may not make sounds or speak.

2) The actor first "tells" the group what kind of pantomime he chose from the hat: a book title, quotation and so forth (see *Common Charade Signals*, for specific directions.)

3) The actor then shows his teammates how many words are in the title or phrase by holding up that many fingers.

It's the actor's choice whether to pantomime the entire title, act out whole words or break words down into their syllables and pantomime these word bits. He can, of course, combine all three methods if his team isn't picking up on his actions.

When the actor's team guesses the title, the play switches

COMMON CHARADE SIGNALS

Book title: Place hands together as if praying, then open them as you would a book.

Play title: Extend one arm out from the chest in a semicircle toward the audience.

Movie title: Make a motion as if holding a movie camera up to your eye. The left hand "holds" the camera while the right hand "turns" the film.

Song title: With hands on either side of your mouth, open your mouth wide as if to call someone or sing loudly.

Quotation, proverb, or phrase: Using the first two fingers of each hand, enclose an imaginary phrase, folding your fingers down twice to draw quotation marks in the air.

Advertising slogan: Use your hands to make a motion of handling money.

Little syllables or little words: Put your thumb and pointer finger together with approximately a half-inch space between them.

Big syllables or big words: Hold your arms apart to indicate the length of the word or syllable. This can be modified to indicate relative lengths.

Past tense: Motion with one hand over the shoulder.

Correct answer: Put your finger to your nose.

to the opposing team. The guessing alternates until the teams go through all the slips of paper.

As a noncompetitive game, the object is just to guess the other team's titles. To keep score, assign a timekeeper—one for each team—to keep track of the opposing team's time (honesty is important here!). The team with the shortest guessing time wins.

Too Close for Comfort

Depending on the makeup of the group, ask couples to pair up or ask the men, the women or half the guests to choose a partner. Give each duo a large uninflated balloon. After each couple blows up the balloon, ties a knot at its neck and positions the balloon at chest height between them, the game is ready to begin. At a predetermined signal, the couples attempt to break the balloon by hugging each other. Whoever breaks the balloon first wins. (Make sure all your guests have removed sharp objects from their jackets, shirts or blouses.)

Another simple game also promotes getting to know each other better. Ask your guests to sit or stand (sitting is more difficult) in a circle. With groups of five or less, use one orange; with groups of up to twelve, use two. Give the oranges to the starters (if using two, hand them to guests who are on opposite sides of the circle) and request that they pass the orange on to the next person in the circle without using their hands. Tuck the orange under the starter's chin. The results are hilarious, especially if one person gets caught with two oranges at the same time. (If this happens and one drops, just let it go; if an orange drops at another time, the guest should pick it up and continue as if nothing happened.)

Taking a Trip

This word game relies on a quick-witted accomplice, someone who will translate your clues into the name of a famous person without—at first—letting anyone else know how he does it. The accomplice leaves the room and you ask your guests to select a personality—John F. Kennedy, for example. Your accomplice reenters the room and you begin a monologue.

"I went on a trip," you say, "where I met a very famous person. First I went to Canada and stayed there for one night before going on to Madrid, where I stayed for two weeks. From there I traveled to Luxembourg for four days and then went to Toronto and rested for a while." At this point your partner may clear his throat or otherwise indicate that he'd like to guess who you met, but you stop him.

"I continued the trip by going first to Portland and then to Reykjavik before spending two days in San Francisco. The next three weeks I hiked around Denmark, then spent two nights in Nice before finishing my trip in Thailand."

Much to your guests' surprise, your accomplice should now step forward and announce that he knows you met JFK in Thailand.

The secrets of the game are simple. Yes, there is a code, but you never spell the name of the person out directly. In this case, I spelled out "Camelot" and "president." (The accomplice may at first have guessed King Arthur, which is why you continued the trip to include the clue "president.") The clues could have been reversed, and if the accomplice can't guess the person from the first trip, you can extend the trip by taking a "rest," which indicates the end of a word, or by announcing that you're taking a "side trip," which more clearly indicates the beginning of a new clue.

Now to the code. The consonants and vowels are encrypted in different ways. To crack the consonant code, listen for the first letter of the geographic destinations (Canada, Madrid, Puerto Rico, San Francisco). The number of hours, days, nights, weeks, or months determines the vowels; according to the A,E,I,O,U system of memorization, assign a number to the vowels, that is, A=1, E=2, I=3, O=4, and U=5. So, if a person travels for *three* nights to *Key West* and then stays for *two* weeks, you can make a pretty good guess that the famous person chosen was Dwight Eisenhower ("Ike"), although in the actual play, "Ike" would not at first be a good clue, because it might be too recognizable. To be good sports, you should make the clues easier as the game goes on, but don't use the person's name directly and never, ever divulge the secret. Once someone in the group guesses the trick, allow her to be your accomplice. The game can become quite frustrating for novices, who may insist the play continues; be forewarned that you may have to invite everyone over the next week to resume the game.

(One last hint: don't fret if you have two vowels in a row. Just embellish; say you spent two days, then decide to stay on for one more day, or say that you spent two weeks and one day.)

Dictionary/Fictionary

No matter what you call this game, it is a gem for small dinner parties, to be played before or after a meal. All that's required is a good dictionary, paper and pens or pencils. One person begins as the leader. She passes out paper and pens to all the guests and explains the game. Basically, she will choose a word from the dictionary that she thinks no one knows. After announcing the word and its spelling—and confirming that all playing are ignorant of its true definition—she writes down the definition on her own slip of paper. As she does this, each person also writes down their own made-up definition and hands it to the leader.

The leader's objective is to stump the crowd, to find a word with a definition that no one will believe. The other players try to invent a definition that their playmates *will* believe.

The game proceeds as the leader reads through all the definitions, at first silently, then out loud. The players may request the leader to reread the definitions before the vote, which can follow in two ways. The leader can go in a circle and ask each player which definition they believe to be true, or she can read each definition a final time and by counting hands record how many people vote for each one.

Each false definition that received a vote scores one point. Each player who guesses the true definition receives one point. The leader scores only if no one guessed the real definition. Round one ends, and the leadership passes on to the next person. By the end of the game, each person should have held the leadership position once.

Cunning players try to outwit their friends by sometimes voting for their own definitions, a strategy that may influence others (although no points are scored for self-votes). One variation outlaws this practice, a rule that the group should establish at the game's outset.

Surprisingly, some of the simplest definitions for the most farfetched words work best, while at other times the craziest definitions are most likely to be believed. There seems to be no pattern to the game except zaniness and fun!

Who Am I? and Botticelli

Who Am I? is the simpler of these two guessing games, based largely on Twenty Questions. In Who Am I? the quizmaster chooses a famous person—living or dead, in history, the arts, fiction and so on—and writes the celebrity's name down on a piece of paper. After announcing the initial of the person's surname (or the name to be recognized), the players ask up to twenty "yes" or "no" questions to elicit facts about the person in question. If the celebrity has not been revealed by the last question, the quizmaster wins and a player takes his place.

In Botticelli, a sophisticated and more competitive version of Who Am I?, the quizmaster also thinks of a person and writes the name down on a piece of paper before telling the players the celebrity's surname initial. The challenge begins immediately.

Suppose the quizmaster chooses Walt Whitman. He announces "W" to the guests, who in an orderly fashion going from left to right or vice versa begin asking specific questions. All of the questions must refer to a person whose surname begins with the same initial as the mystery celebrity.

"Are you an American president?" the first player asks. The quizmaster replies, "No, I am not George Washington."

"Are you another American President?" the second player asks.

"No, I am not Woodrow Wilson," says the quizmaster.

"Are you the author of *Mrs. Dalloway*?"

"No, I am not Virginia Woolf."

And the play proceeds until the quizmaster is stumped, or until someone guesses the name.

"Are you a famous children's book author who also wrote for *The New Yorker* magazine?"

The quizmaster can't remember the name of E.B. White so he gives in and the player who asked the stumper now gets to ask the quizmaster a "yes" or "no" question: "Is the person a female?" is usually the first question. The second: "Is the person living?"

What becomes the most fun is when a player asks a question such as "Are you a famous female American writer sympathetic to the constrictions of women in the early twentieth century?" having in mind Edith Wharton, yet the quizmaster responds, "No, I am not Eudora Welty." Welty doesn't quite fit the definition, having established her career later in the century; the group must then decide whether to allow the player a "yes" or "no" question.

Botticelli can captivate a roomful of people for hours, but if not everyone is absorbed, it can also drag on for some guests; setting a time or question limit to the game solves the problem.

WALT WHITMAN

WOODROW WILSON

EUDORA WELTY

VIRGINIA WOOLF

EDITH WHARTON

E. B. WHITE

GEORGE WASHINGTON

January 19 Antarctica discovered, 1840

February 7 Beatles arrived in the U.S., 1964

March 5 Fifth day of National Peanut Month

May 29 John F. Kennedy born, 1917

June 18 International Picnic Day

July 16 National Ice Cream Week continues

September 9 Chrysanthemum Day in Japan

October 3 Third day of National Apple Month

REWARD
(\$5,000.00)
Reward for the capture, dead or alive of one Wm. Wright, better known as
"BILLY THE KID"

November 23 Billy the Kid born, 1859

April 3 First Pony Express delivery, 1860

August 21 Count Basie born, 1904

December 16 Beethoven born, 1770

CALENDAR OF PARTY EXCUSES

This Calendar of Party Excuses offers solutions for everyone who's tired of hosting the same kinds of parties over and over. Think how happy your guests would be if they arrived at your party in late December and instead of another Christmas get-together complete with green and red wreaths and scented candles, they walked into a celebration of the Mexican Night of the Radishes, with mariachi music, spicy food and colorful decorations.

What follows are 365 great ways to avoid indecision. It's impossible to find a single day that doesn't offer some reason to have a small party, whether it's the commemoration of a political event, a famous birthday or a festival borrowed from another culture or religion. Once you choose the initial reason to celebrate, spend a few minutes at the library planning the party. Start by looking in an encyclopedia and then if you need more information, ask the reference librarian for help.

Once you have some background information, figure out an innovative way to share it with your guests. For instance, if you're going to celebrate the Elgin, South Carolina, Catfish Stomp, you might want to look up the South Carolina flag and use its colors when decorating; look in the music library for some bluegrass music—especially any songs about catfish; and serve catfish, or other fish dressed up with carrot sliver "whiskers."

Whatever occasion you choose to celebrate, have fun and don't be afraid to follow your imagination to it's most interesting conclusions. Your guests will be happy, and your party will be a great success.

January

1 Feast of Fools
2 Ancestry Day in Haiti
3 Alaska admitted to the Union, 1959
4 Quadrantid meteor shower
5 Twelfth Night
6 Four Freedoms Day
7 Man Watchers' Week begins
8 Elvis Presley born, 1935
9 Joan Baez born, 1941
10 Order of the Golden Fleece founded, 1429
11 *Romeo and Juliet* opened in Leningrad, 1940
12 Charles Perrault born, 1628
13 Robert C. Weaver became the first black man in the U.S. Cabinet, 1966
14 Telephone first shown to Queen Victoria, 1878
15 Martin Luther King, Jr., born, 1929
16 Prohibition Day
17 Robert Scott reached the South Pole, 1912
18 A.A. Milne born, 1882
19 Antarctica discovered, 1840
20 St. Agnes' Eve
21 Lowcountry Oyster Festival in Charleston, SC
22 Feast Day of St. Vincent of Saragossa, patron saint of wine growers
23 Iceland's Eldfell volcano erupted, 1973
24 Gold discovered in California, 1848
25 Robert Burns' Night in Scotland
26 *Der Rosenkavalier* opened in Dresden
27 St. Devota day, in Monaco
28 U.S. Coast Guard established, 1915
29 American Baseball League formed, 1900
30 The lone ranger radio debut, 1933
31 Feast Day of St. John Basco, patron saint of editors

February

1 Potato Lovers' Month begins
2 Candlemas
3 Bean Throwing Night in Japan
4 George Washington elected president, 1789
5 Spring Festival in Mauritius
6 Middle of Carrot Festival Days in Holtville, CA
7 Beatles arrived in the U.S. for the first time, 1964
8 Narvik Sun Festival in Norway
9 Gasparilla Pirate Festival in Tampa, FL
10 Beginning of the Citrus Festival in Winter Haven, FL
11 National Inventors Day
12 Hawaii's King Kalakaua and Queen Kapiolani coronated, 1883
13 Abraham Lincoln born, 1809
14 Valentine's Day
15 Lupercalia
16 King Tut's tomb opened, 1924
17 *Madame Butterfly* premiered in Milan, 1904
18 The planet Pluto discovered, 1930
19 Omega-minus subatomic particle detected, 1964
20 John Glenn became first American to orbit Earth, 1962
21 Romanov reign began in Russia, 1613
22 Popcorn introduced to the colonists, 1630
23 W.E.B. Dubois born, 1868
24 The republic of France proclaimed, 1848
25 Magna Carta issued in final form, 1225
26 Grand Canyon established as a national park, 1919
27 Pancake Day in Liberal, KS
28 First killer whale born in captivity, 1977

March

1 Yellowstone became a national park, 1872
2 First National Basketball Association All-Star Game played, 1951
3 Peach Festival and Doll's Day in Japan
4 Fourth day of National Procrastination Week
5 Fifth day of National Peanut Month
6 Valentina Vladimirovna became first woman in space, 1963
7 Victor Company issued first jazz recording, 1917
8 International Women's Day
9 Baron Bliss Day in Belize
10 First clear sentence transmitted over the telephone, 1876
11 Johnny Appleseed day
12 Great Blizzard hit northeast U.S., 1888
13 The planet Uranus discovered, 1781
14 Albert Einstein born, 1879
15 Ides of March
16 Barnum and Bailey circus had its debut in New York City, 1881
17 St. Patrick's Day
18 Whale Festival in Mendocino, CA
19 Swallows fly back to the Mission of San Juan Capistrano, CA
20 Ovid born, 43 B.C.
21 Vernal equinox
22 Equal Rights Amendment passed by U.S. Senate, 1972
23 World Meteorological Day
24 Harry Houdini born, 1874
25 Maryland Day
26 Regatta Day in Hawaii
27 International Theater Day in the U.S.S.R.
28 Three Mile Island nuclear power plant malfunctions and shuts down, 1979
29 Vietnam Veteran's day
30 Alaska bought for $7,200,000 in 1867
31 Dalai Lama safely entered into exile in India, 1959

April

1 April Fool's Day
2 Tater Day in Benton, KY
3 First Pony Express delivery leaves Missouri for California, 1860
4 NATO established, 1949
5 Pocahontas and John Smith married, 1614
6 Reagan agreed to acid-rain talks, 1987
7 Women's day in Mozambique
8 Gautama Buddha's day of birth and enlightenment
9 Golf Hall of Fame established, 1941
10 ASPCA founded, 1866
11 Napoleon exiled to Elba, 1814
12 Yuri Gagarin became first man to orbit Earth, 1961
13 Handel's *Messiah* premiered in Dublin, 1742
14 Chicken Strut in Bethune, SC
15 Good Roads day in Illinois
16 Giant panda given to National Zoo, 1972
17 Thornton Wilder born, 1897
18 Paul Revere's and William Dawes' rides, 1775
19 Oxford English Dictionary completed, 1928
20 Napoleon Bonaparte born, 1808
21 Lyrid meteor shower
22 Earth Day
23 Peppercorn Day in Bermuda
24 Library of Congress established, 1800
25 Feast of St. Mark, patron of Venice, glaziers, and lawyers
26 Christening date of William Shakespeare, 1564
27 National Whistlers Convention in Louisburg, NC
28 Arbor Day
29 National Trout Festival in Kalkaska, MI
30 Walpurgis Night

May

1 Lei Day in Hawaii
2 Second day of National Barbecue Month
3 Richard D'Oyly Carte born, 1844, and Pete Seeger born, 1919
4 Cricket Day in Italy
5 Kentucky Derby
6 Shad Festival in Bethlehem, PA
7 Radio Day in the U.S.S.R.
8 Cornwall's Furry Day and V-E Day
9 Church condemnation of Galileo Galilei reversed, 1983
10 Second Continental Congress opened in Philadelphia, 1775
11 Constantinople founded, 330
12 International Bar-B-Q Festival in Owensboro, KY
13 Mother's Day
14 Skylab launched, 1973
15 Peace Officers' Memorial Day
16 Samuel Johnson and James Boswell met, 1763
17 World Telecommunications Day
18 Calaveras County Fair and Jumping Frog Jubilee in Angels Camp, CA
19 Kenya banned big-game hunting, 1977
20 Vidalia Onion Festival in Vidalia, GA
21 Asternarides Feast
22 National Maritime Day
23 Carolus Linnaeus born, 1707
24 Amy Johnson became first woman to fly solo from England to Australia, 1930
25 Africa Freedom Day
26 Apricot Fiesta in Patterson, CA
27 Amelia Bloomer, Wild Bill Hickock, Isadora Duncan and Rachel Carson born
28 Dionne quintuplets born, 1934
29 John F. Kennedy born in Brookline, MA, 1917
30 First Indy 500 race, 1911
31 End of Pickle Week

June

1 National Dairy Month begins
2 Elizabeth II coronated, 1953
3 Milk Day Festival in Harvard IL
4 Parsi Festival of Wine, Garlic and Meat
5 World Environment Day
6 Mount McKinley (Denali) first ascended, 1913
7 Paul Gaugin born, 1848
8 Frank Lloyd Wright born, 1867
9 North Carolina's Blue Crab Derby and Festival in Morehead City
10 Delmarva Chicken Festival in Milford, DE
11 *Gossamer Albatross* made the first man-powered flight across the English Channel, 1979
12 Comstock Lode discovered, 1859
13 Miranda Decision, 1966
14 Bastille Day
15 Magna Carta signed, 1215
16 Alabama Blueberry Festival in Brewton
17 Igor Stravinsky born, 1882
18 International Picnic Day
19 Father's Day first observed, 1910
20 Louis XVI and Marie Antoinette try to leave France in disguise, 1791
21 Berry-Dairy Days in Burlington, WA
22 Richard II crowned, 1377
23 Anniversary of Iceland's Alting, the oldest parliament in the world
24 Midsummer's Day
25 First commercial color television program telecast
26 U.N. Charter Day
27 Emma Goldman born, 1869
28 Mel Brooks born, 1926
29 Seychelles Independence day
30 Watermelon Thump in Luling, TX

July

1   First Day of July Belongs to Blueberries day
2   Il Palio
3   Third day of National Hot Dog Month
4   Independence Day and Indian Rights Day in Wisconsin
5   Heroes Day in Zambia
6   First transatlantic dirigible crossing, 1919
7   Vega Star Festival in Japan
8   Beginning of National Cherry Festival in Traverse City, MI
9   Nikola Tesla born, 1856
10   Feast of Fortune in Japan
11   Five-billionth baby born, 1987
12   Henry VIII and Catherine Parr married, 1542
13   Live Aid, 1985
14   Aborigine's Day in Australia
15   St. Swithin's Day
16   National Ice Cream Week continues
17   Feast of the Redeemer in Venice
18   Railroad Day
19   First woman's rights convention held at Seneca Falls, NY, 1848
20   International Chess Day in the U.S.S.R.
21   Gilroy Garlic Festival in Gilroy, CA
22   Maria Spelterina crossed over Niagara Falls on a tightrope, 1876
23   Raymond Chandler and Haile Selassie born, 1888 and 1892
24   Alexandre Dumas born, 1802
25   First test-tube baby born, 1978
26   St. Anne's Day
27   The Original Lobster Festival begins in Rockland, ME
28   Beatrix Potter born, 1866
29   Charles, Prince of Wales, and Lady Diana Spencer married, 1981
30   The first representative assembly in America met at Jamestown, VA, 1619
31   Edison granted phonograph patent, 1877

August

1   Lammas Day
2   Picnic Day in Northern Territory, Australia
3   American Canoe Association organized, 1880
4   Pueblo Corn Dance
5   Klamath Salmon Festival and Boat Races in Klamath, CA
6   First woman swam across the English Channel, 1926
7   Nixon resigned, 1974
8   First ascent of Mt. Blanc, 1786
9   Beginning of Australian gold rush, 1851
10   Idaho's Huckleberry Festival begins
11   Popcorn Festival in Van Buren, IN
12   Perseid meteor shower
13   Annie Oakley born, 1860
14   Macbeth became King of Scots, 1040
15   Woodstock Music and Art Fair held in Bethel, NY, 1969
16   Klondike gold rush started at Bonanza Creek, 1896
17   The *Double Eagle II* became first helium-filled balloon to cross the Atlantic, 1978
18   Crow Fair in Montana
19   *Yip, Yip, Yaphank* had its debut at Camp Upton, NY, 1918
20   Reinhold Messner first to climb Mt. Everest solo, 1980
21   Count Basie born, 1904
22   Dorothy Parker and Ray Bradbury born, 1893 and 1920
23   Gene Kelly born, 1912
24   Mt. Vesuvius erupted, burying Pompeii and Herculaneum, 79
25   U.S. National Park Service established
26   Navy's Cheever Felch saw a sea serpent, 1819
27   Lyndon B. Johnson born, 1908
28   Palace of Peace dedicated at the Hague, 1913
29   First Opium War ended, 1842
30   Hot line established between Washington and Moscow, 1963
31   First All-Star Football Game, 1934

September

1   Apache Sunrise Dance
2   V-J Day, 1945
3   Labor Day
4   Mark Spitz won seven gold medals in the 1972 Olympics
5   Be Late for Something Day
6   Somhlolo Day in Swaziland
7   World Kielbasa Festival begins in Chicopee, MA
8   National Rub a Bald Head Week begins
9   Chrysanthemum Day in Japan
10   Swap Ideas Day
11   O. Henry (William Sydney Porter) born, 1862
12   Defender's Day
13   Rhinoceros first brought to New York City, 1826
14   Gregorian calendar adopted in England, 1752
15   Festivals Acadiens in Lafayette, LA
16   National Play-Doh Day
17   Constitution Day
18   Ukelele patented, 1917
19   International Day of Peace
20   Billie Jean King defeated Bobby Riggs, 1973
21   Stonehenge sold to C.H.E. Chubb for approximately $6,600 in 1915
22   Ice cream patent filed, 1903
23   First baseball team organized, 1845
24   Supreme Court created, 1789
25   Glenn Gould born, 1932
26   *West Side Story* opened in New York City, 1957
27   Samuel Adams born, 1722
28   Confucius born
29   Michaelmas day
30   Last day of the Oyster Festival in Oyster Bay, NY

October

1 Roger Maris broke Babe Ruth's record, 1961
2 It's Pizza Festival Time
3 Third day of National Apple Month
4 Dick Tracy debuted, 1931
5 International Balloon Fiesta begins in Albuquerque, NM
6 Universal Children's Day
7 The World Enchilada Festival in Las Cruces, NM
8 Great Chicago Fire, 1871
9 Korean Alphabet Day
10 Alberto Giacometti and Thelonius Monk born, 1901 and 1918
11 Eleanor Roosevelt born, 1884
12 Christopher Columbus first landed in the New World, 1492
13 Peanut Festival in Suffolk, VA
14 Brussels Sprouts Festival in Santa Cruz, CA
15 World Poetry Day
16 World Food Day
17 Black Poetry Day
18 Alaska Day
19 Auguste Lumiere, co-inventor of the motion picture, born in 1862
20 Woolly Worm Festival in Banner Elk, NC
21 Orionid meteor shower
22 Ravel's Bolero premiered in Paris, 1928
23 Kellerton, KS, hosted the first national horseshoe pitching contest, 1915
24 United Nations Day
25 Minnie Pearl born, 1912
26 Erie Canal opened, 1825
27 Georgia Sweet Potato Festival in Ocilla
28 Grover Cleveland dedicated the Statue of Liberty, 1886
29 Bela Lugosi born, 1884
30 Orson Welles broadcast War of the Worlds, 1939
31 Halloween

November

1 All Saint's Day
2 Daniel Boone born, 1734
3 Cheese Festival in Watonga, SD
4 Kona Coffee Festival in Kailua-Kona, HI
5 Guy Fawkes' Day
6 Election Day
7 Republican elephant cartoon debut, 1874
8 Feast of the Four Crowned Ones
9 Great Blackout in the northeastern U.S. and Canada, 1965
10 World Youth Day in the U.S.S.R.
11 Veteran's Day
12 Sun Yat-sen born, 1866
13 Walt Disney's Fantasia first movie to use stereophonic sound, 1940
14 First American golf club organized in Yonkers, NY, 1888
15 Zebulon Pike first saw the mountain peak named after him, 1806
16 Sound of Music opened in New York City, 1959
17 Sadie Hawkins Day
18 Steamboat Willie premiered as first animated cartoon talkie
19 Abraham Lincoln delivered the Gettysburg Address, 1863
20 USDA halted use of DDT in residential areas
21 Mayflower Compact signed, 1620
22 Thanksgiving Day
23 Billy the Kid born, 1859
24 Collard Festival in Ponce de Leon, FL
25 Ragtime great Willie Smith born, 1897
26 Charles Schultz born, 1922
27 Treaty of Neuilly ended World War I, 1919
28 Independence Proclamation Day in Albania
29 Richard Byrd flew over the South Pole, 1929
30 Floyd Patterson defeated Archie Moore to become heavyweight champ, 1959

December

1 Catfish Stomp in Elgin, SC
2 Napoleon Bonaparte crowned Emperor of France, 1804
3 First successful human heart transplant, 1967
4 Day of the Artisans in Mexico
5 Stop the Draft demonstration in New York City, 1967
6 Ira Gershwin born, 1896
7 Steam locomotive first used in Germany, 1835
8 First U.S. pro football game broadcast on radio, 1940
9 John Milton born, 1608
10 Human Rights Day
11 UNICEF established
12 Crossword puzzle day
13 Soot Sweeping Day in Japan
14 Roald Amundsen first reached the South Pole, 1911
15 Bill of Rights adopted, 1791
16 Beethoven born, 1770
17 Saturnalia
18 Thirteenth Amendment, prohibiting slavery, ratified, 1863
19 Princess Bernice Pauahi Bishop, of Hawaii, born (year unknown)
20 Louisiana Territory incorporated into the United States, 1803
21 First crossword puzzle printed in a New York paper, 1913
22 International Arbor Day
23 Night of the Radishes in Mexico
24 Eugene Debs pardoned, 1921
25 George Washington crossed the Delaware, 1776
26 Boxing Day
27 Radio City Music Hall in New York City opened, 1932
28 Comet Kohoutek was closest to the sun, 1973
29 Texas admitted to the Union, 1845
30 Joseph Rudyard Kipling born, 1865
31 Hogmanay Day in Scotland

Sources

Breads

Dimpflmeier Bakery
19 Jutland Road
Toronto, Canada M8Z 2G6
(416) 253-5554
(800) 387-8702
*German breads, including sourdough,
pumpernickel and rye*

Wolferman's
8900 Marshall Drive
PO Box 15913
Lenexa, Kansas 66215
(800) 255-0169
(913) 432-6131
Oversized English muffins and breakfast foods

Caviar

Caspian Caviar
PO Box 876
Highland Mill
Camden, Maine 04843
(207) 236-4436

Poriloff American Sturgeon Caviar
47-39 49th Street
Woodside, New York 11377
(718) 784-3344

Cheeses

Ideal Cheese Shop
1205 Second Avenue
New York, New York 10021
(212) 688-7579
Various cheeses

Maytag Dairy Farm
Box 806
Newton, Iowa 50208
(800) 247-2458
(800) 258-2437
Specialize in blue cheese

Shelburne Farms
Junction of Harbor and Bay Roads
Shelburne, Vermont 05482
(802) 985-8686
Farmhouse Cheddar cheese

Chocolates and Desserts

Buckley's English Toffee, Inc.
Box 14119
Baton Rouge, LA 70898-4119
(504) 642-8381
Chocolates and desserts

Champlain Chocolate Company
431 Pine Street
Burlington, VT 05401
(802) 864-1808
American truffles

Polly Jean's Pantry
4561 Mission Gorge Place, Suite K
San Diego, CA 92120
(800) 882-7323 or (619) 283-5429
Chocolate and fruit dessert sauces

Teuscher Chocolates of Switzerland
620 Fifth Avenue
New York, NY 10020
(212) 246-4416
Swiss truffles

Fruits and Vegetables

The El Paso Chile Company™
100 Ruhlin Court
El Paso, TX 79922
(915) 544-3434
*Dried and canned chilies, salsa, and other
Mexican foods*

Kraft-Rosenblum
2101 91st Street
North Bergen, NJ 07017
(201) 854-1100
Fresh produce and seafood

Genovesi Food Company
PO Box 5668
Dayton, OH 45405
(513) 277-2173
Sundried tomatoes

Harry and David
Bear Creek Orchards
2581 South Pacific Coast Highway
Medford, OR 97501
(503) 776-2400
Fresh fruit

Mission Orchards
2296 Sentral Road
San Jose, CA 95112
(408) 297-5056
Fresh fruit and specialty foods

Paradise Farms
PO Box 436
Summerland, CA 93067
(805) 684-9468
Edible flowers

Santa Barbara Olive Company, Inc.
1661 Mission Drive
Solvang, CA 93463
(805) 688-9917
Olives

Sarabeth's Kitchen
423 Amsterdam Avenue
New York, NY 10024
(212) 496-6280
Jams, preserves and fruit butters

Herbs and Spices

Rathdowney Herbs Limited
3 River Street
PO Box 357
Bethel, VT 05032
(802) 234-5157
Various herbs and spices

United Society of Shakers
Poland Spring, ME 04274
(207) 926-4597
Various herbs and spices

Solly's Choice
3814 Fourth Avenue South
Seattle, WA 98134
(206) 624-7280
Windowsill herb gardens

The Herbfarm
32804 Issaquah-Fall City Road
Fall City, WA 98024
(206) 784-2222
Windowsill herb gardens

Indoor Grilling Equipment

Zona
97 Greene Street
New York, NY 10012
(212) 925-6750
West Village forge fireplace grill

Meats, Poultry and Game

D'Artagnan, Inc.
399-419 St. Paul's Avenue
Jersey City, NJ 07306
(800) DARTAGNAN or (201) 792-0748
Foie gras

Lawrence's Smoke House
Route 30
Townshend, VT 05359
(802) 365-7372
Corncob-smoked ham

Meadow Farms Country Smokehouse
PO Box 1387
Bishop, CA 93514
(619) 873-5311
Mahogany-smoked ham

Smithfield Ham & Products Co.
PO Box 487
Smithfield, VA 23430
(800) 628-2242 or (804) 357-2121
Dry-smoked, salt-cured ham

S. Wallace Edwards & Sons, Inc.
Box 25
Surry, VA 23883
(800) 222-4267 or (804) 294-3121
Hickory-smoked ham

Wild Game Inc.
2315 West Huron Street
Chicago, IL 60612
(312) 944-2607
Game

Oils, Vinegars and Mustards

Duggan's Ingredients
1365-A Interior Street
Eugene, OR 97402
(503) 343-8697

The Silver Palate
274 Columbus Avenue
New York, NY 10023
(800) 847-4747 or (212) 799-6340

Various Ingredients and Equipment

American Spoon Foods
PO Box 566
Petoskey, MI 49770
(616) 347-9030

Dean & DeLuca Mail-Order Department
110 Greene Street, Suite 304
New York, NY 10012
(212) 431-1691

Market Square Food Company
1642 Richfield Avenue
Highland Park, IL 60035
(800) 232-2299 or (312) 831-2228

Williams-Sonoma Catalogue
Box 7456
San Francisco, CA 94120-7456
(415) 421-4242

Zabar's
2245 Broadway
New York, NY 10024
(212) 787-2000

Wild Rice

Northern Lakes Wild Rice Company
P.O. Box 592
Teton Village, Wyoming 83025
(307) 733-7.192

Index

Additional photography credits:

© Joy Brenner/FPG International: 31 © Burke/Triolo: 33, 69, 93, 118 © Bruce Byers/FPG International: 41 bottom right © FPG International: 89, 121 © Michael Grand: 28 © Jerry Howard/Positive Images: 33 © James Krajicek: 98 © Brian Leatart: 48 © Robert Lima/Envision: 66 © Banus March/FPG International: 30 © Felicia Martinez/PhotoEdit: 16, 17, 42 © Melabee Miller/Envision: 128 © Steven Mark Needham/Envision: 58, 73, 84, 90, 116 North Wind Picture Archives: 114 © Guy Powers/Envision: 43, 97 © Terry Wild: 96 Courtesy Williams-Sonoma: 16, 17, 104

Page 132: Row one (left to right): © Tim Gibson/Envision, UPI/Bettmann Newsphotos, © FPG International, North Wind Picture Archives Row two: © UPI/Bettmann Newsphotos, © Tom Tracy/FPG International © Simon Metz/FPG International, UPI/Bettmann Newsphotos Row three: © Dick Pietrzyk/FPG International, © Gordon E. Smith, UPI/Bettman Newsphotos, North Wind Picture Archives